Old Lifeboat Station
Blakeney Point

The Vikings

Church ~ Salthouse

W ✦ E

S

Windmill
Cley next the Sea

Elephant ~ West Runton

Black Shuck

Morston
Blakeney
Cley next the Sea
Salthouse
Weybourne
Upper Sheringham
Sheringham
West Runton
East Runton
Cromer

ELEMENTS OF THE
NORTH NORFOLK COAST

WILDLIFE VILLAGES HISTORY MYTHS AND LEGENDS

David North and Martin Hayward Smith

ELEMENTS OF THE
NORTH NORFOLK COAST

WILDLIFE VILLAGES HISTORY MYTHS AND LEGENDS

Author: David North   Photographer: Martin Hayward Smith

Limited First Edition of 5000 copies

Opposite: Freedom is space, space is freedom. West Sands at low tide looking towards East Hills, Wells-next-the-Sea.   Above: Sunset at Brancaster Staithe.

Published by Birdseyeview Books
Villa Farm, Thurgarton, Norwich, Norfolk, NR11 7PD.
www.birdseyeviewbooks.com

First published: 2004

Author: David North
Photographer: Martin Hayward Smith
www.martinhaywardsmith.co.uk
Endpaper artwork: Prunella Van der Hoorn

Dedication: Martin Hayward Smith

To my father who shines down upon me, and to Megan
(Little Breeches) – for over a rainbow the world's one big
sandcastle.

Dedication: David North

To my wife, Tasha, with love. You open my heart to the
magic of life. Your love anchors me in shifting sands and
storms and lets me fly on starry nights. Special places
become more special shared with you.

ISBN: 0-9547927-0-X

Design, layout, reprographics, printing and binding by
Butler and Tanner Limited, Frome and London

Right: **Pines at East Hills, Wells-next-the-Sea.**

CONTENTS

ELEMENTS OF THE NORTH NORFOLK COAST

INTRODUCTION

The only thing constant on this coast is change. Tides sweep in and out over the huge open sands of Holkham bay. They swirl up and down sinuously-winding muddy channels at Morston, and ooze out again leaving glistening mud for beaks to probe and geese to leave their footprints in. Waves breathe in and out, sighing against Cley shingle and displacing seals from their slumbers on Blakeney sand bars. Storms sweep in off the North Sea and gnaw away at Weybourne and Runton cliffs, changing geography in a night.

This play of light and tide, wind and wave, changes not just daily but quite literally from moment to moment. You can never walk the same beach twice, part of the magic that makes this coast so special. The coast responds to many rhythms: twice daily tides, the monthly lunar cycles of springs and neaps, and the changing seasons. These bring a different kind of tide – tides of birds which ebb and flow across continents making North Norfolk their international meeting place. Autumn geese in skeins fill skies with their sound, spring swallows twist and turn over reedbed and marsh before vanishing inland over sea walls with an energy which belies their 6000 mile journey to reach our shore.

There are rhythms which are so beyond our human time scales that to us they remain largely hidden, though their reality is written in coastal geography.

The tides of climate change once brought tropical seas to cover the land here, allowing the chalk which underlies this coast to form. During the Ice Age great glacial tides of ice deposited the sands, gravels and flints that form the soft cliffs of Weybourne to Cromer and Norfolk's hill country, the Cromer Ridge.

The North Norfolk coastline is loved by many people – people who live and work along this coast, people who travel many hundreds of miles to birdwatch here and the thousands who holiday here. This is a book for anyone who has a relationship with this unique area, a celebration of just some of its qualities, and a quirky but hopefully fascinating look at its wildlife, history and villages. The coast will continue to change but, with the care of all who visit, its beauty and magic will remain.

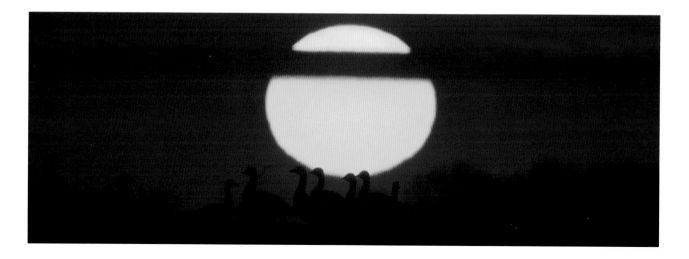

Opposite: **Dawn at Morston creek.** Above: **Pink-footed geese at sunset – Brancaster.**

8

The underlying character of the North Norfolk coast is rooted in the rocks and sediments which in their various combinations create an amazing diversity of landscapes. Chalk and flint, sand and shingle, mud and clay. These are the bones and body of the coast: clothed by nature with dune flowers and the greys, greens and browns of saltmarsh plants; and by man with his crops of beet, barley and wheat.

Equally, the impact of the glaciers and ice sheets which have come and gone over the last two million years has been profound. We simplify this complex period of alternating warm and cold conditions by terming it the Ice Age. Yet any walk below the cliffs that run from Weybourne to Cromer and beyond can only awe us with the scale and volume of sands, gravels, muds and clays which are the legacy of this period. North Norfolk's 'uplands', which lie inland from Cromer and Sheringham, are created by a ridge of sands and gravels deposited along the melting edge of a former ice sheet.

The chalk which underlies the whole of the North Norfolk coast, and indeed much of East Anglia, is a generally hidden presence. Apart from the magnificent Hunstanton cliffs, it rarely shouts its presence but its influence on man and nature is pervasive. The surface of every ploughed field in North Norfolk is littered with flints eroded from the upper chalk, and for millennia people have made use of their unique qualities. Their sharp glassy edges when knapped could even be said to have changed the course of human evolution, as without the use of flint tools our history would surely have taken a different direction. For centuries untold people have collected flints for making roads, cobbled pathways and buildings. North Norfolk is the land of flint. The history and character of our coastal villages are not just set in stone – they are set in flint.

Left: **Chalk outcrop – Hunstanton cliffs.**
Opposite: **Flints on West Runton beach – looking east towards Cromer pier.**

Mackerel sky and mare's tails
Make tall ships carry low sails
(Trad.)

Out on the marshes, or along the beaches and
cliffs of North Norfolk, the sky and clouds are
as much part of the experience as the landscape.
The strength and direction of the wind are
determining factors for both people and wildlife.

The awesome power of the wind can push
tides more than two metres higher than predicted.
A northerly gale combined with spring tides can
rework the coast in storm surges that several
times a century have wrought destruction on
villages along the coast.

For sailors and fishermen, keeping an eye
on the barometer and reading the signs in the
sky are matters of survival. Head north from
the North Norfolk coast and there is no land
between here and the Arctic Circle. A northerly
gale can lay an icy arctic hand on this coast and
fling itself at you with the force generated by
a thousand cold miles of sea crossing. This is
Norfolk's famed lazy wind that blows through
you, not round you!

Opposite: **Storm brewing over farmland at Barsham.**
Right: **Wind-etched clouds – North Norfolk coast.**

Symbol of energy

Sunrise and sunset, summer solstice and winter solstice – these are the great daily and seasonal fire cycles of the sun that pull the tides of life on the coast. Tides of migratory birds ebb and flow with the seasons: warblers, swallows and terns in spring; and the great skeins of geese in autumn. Dawn and dusk, when the world holds its breath between day and night, are times when the power and magic of this coast are felt most strongly.

Throughout history man has used fire to tame parts of the land here. Coastal heathlands were traditionally managed by burning. This encouraged a flush of new growth for sheep to graze and prevented trees and scrub encroaching. North Norfolk's heaths are no longer managed by fire but some coastal reedbeds are still burnt. Burning the reeds in winter helps prevent an accumulation of dead material which, if left, can gradually lead to the reedbed drying out.

Fire is both a creative force and a destructive one. The pinewoods at Holkham and Wells have both suffered damage from accidental fires. Gorse-covered heaths at Kelling and Salthouse are also prone to fire damage, whether deliberately lit by vandals, or perhaps accidentally caused by the sun's rays on a carelessly discarded glass bottle.

Right: **Blacksmith – North Creake.**
Opposite: **Reed burning at Cley Marshes – January.**

WATER

One element but with so many moods. There are evenings when a spring tide creeps over the marshes so calmly and gently that the water lies like glass, a mirror without a ripple. There are winter storms which hurl themselves against the Weybourne to Cromer cliffs, pushing the land back in places by metres in a single night, and transporting millions of tons of material into the North Sea in a few short hours.

Whether for fishing in, sailing on, or paddling through, it's water, the most mutable of elements, that draws us to the coast.

Opposite: **Reflections – dawn at Blakeney Point.**
Below: **Shelducks over winter waves – off Cromer beach.**

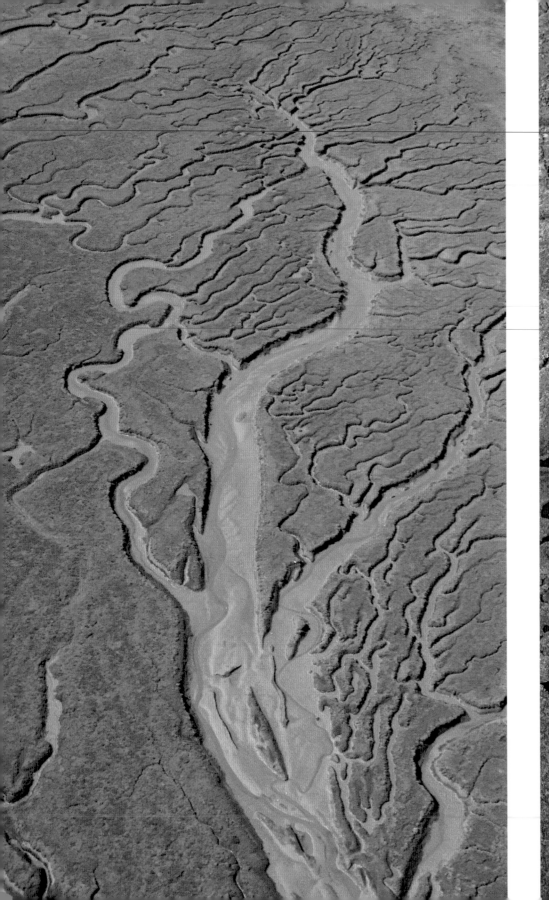
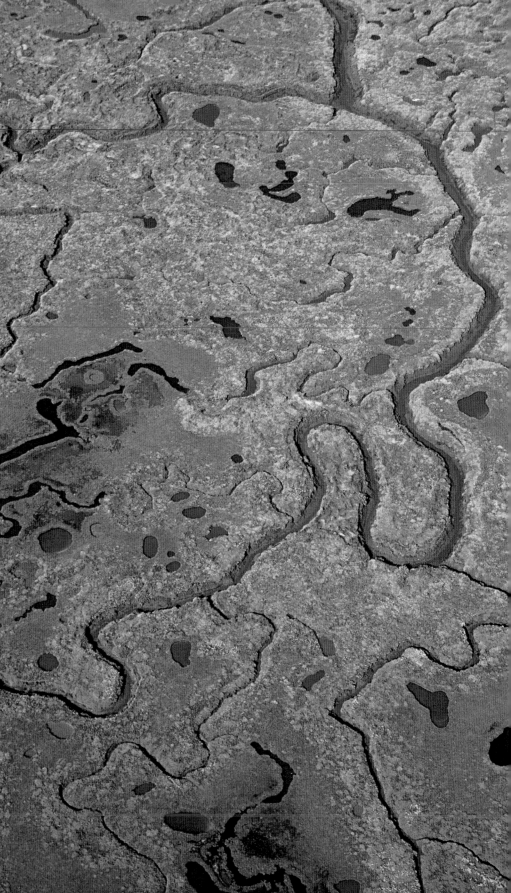

Beyond the margins of the land tamed by man lies an open wilderness, a place of sinuously-winding creeks in mysterious patterns written by the tide. Ebb tide reveals silver pools, magical marsh-mirrors reflecting only sky and clouds, their silences broken by hauntingly beautiful calls – redshank, curlew and in winter, the whistling of wigeon and murmurings of brent. For these birds saltmarsh is home, a familiar place of refuge and safety. Venturing into their world, our senses sharpen in the exhilaration of wide horizons heightened by aloneness and the awareness that for us there is danger here. This is the birds' home and I am the stranger, envious of their freedom but always drawn back to experience these wild open spaces of soft browns and greens with the smell of salt on the wind and the ever-changing light and tide.

Extensive saltmarshes fringe the Wash and extend along the North Norfolk coast between Holme and Blakeney Point. They are at their greatest extent between Thornham and Burnham Overy, and between Wells and Blakeney.

Opposite left: **Saltmarsh patterns – winding creek near Brancaster.**

Opposite right: **Saltmarsh patterns – Stiffkey marshes from the air.**

Above: **Saltmarsh pan – winter frost at Warham marshes.**

18

Glistening wet mud reflects the sun and the sky. For a few magical moments dark mudflats are transformed into dazzling silver or in the warm light of sunset turn to burnished copper. As the tide turns, creeping along the winding creeks and channels, it rises, at first almost imperceptibly and then with increasing speed, covering the mudflats. These areas are never silent. The mud has its own vocabulary of watery noises as the incoming tide forces air out of its pores – from lugworm and ragworm burrows and the hidden underworlds of cockle and mussel beds.

As the tide moves so do the wader flocks which probe the mud for rich pickings. In the distance, wings catch the light one moment and vanish the next, so that whole flocks of waders, like shoals of silver fish, appear and disappear as they twist and turn. The strident piping of oystercatchers, whistles of redshank, mournful callings of grey plover and spine-tingling bubbling trills of curlew, capture perfectly the wildness and isolation of these places. For all their apparent barrenness, muddy areas are more productive than any other coastal habitat. They are an essential element in supporting the vast numbers of migratory waders and wildfowl which for much of the year make this coast so special.

The most extensive mudflats on the Norfolk coast are found on the Wash. Other tidal mudflats occur between Brancaster and Scolt Head Island, in the estuary of the River Burn at Burnham Overy Staithe and in the areas between Morston, Blakeney and Blakeney Point. Throughout the North Norfolk saltmarshes the network of tidal creeks and channels provides further vital muddy feeding grounds for waders and wildfowl.

Above: **Waders over Wash mudflats.**
Opposite: **Burnham Overy creek at low tide.**

Walk the coastal ridge between Weybourne, Salthouse and Cley, or the three-mile spit of Blakeney Point, and even with your eyes shut you will have no doubts whatsoever that you are on shingle. The distinctive crunch of shingle underfoot and the heaviness of every step, mark out the shingle coastline as different. Walk a mile on shingle and it feels like three!

While loose shingle is an inhospitable environment for plants, some specialised species are well-adapted to grow here. Yellow horned-poppy, sea campion, docks and the rare sea kale make their home on shingle. Their seeds provide food in autumn and early winter for linnets, goldfinches, twite and snow buntings.

Sit on the shingle ridge anywhere between Weybourne and Blakeney Point and watch passing terns diving for small fish in summer or look for divers, auks and sea ducks in winter. If you grow tired of sea-watching then simply enjoy the distinctive roar and sigh of breaking waves on shingle or spend a few minutes searching the pebbles for attractive stones – a sea-polished agate or a milky white quartz will not be difficult to find.

Extensive shingle beach areas run from Cromer below the cliffs to Weybourne and then form the distinctive beach ridge which extends seven miles from Weybourne to Blakeney Point. This ridge has been bulldozed higher to act as a sea defence between Salthouse and Cley but then takes its natural form – broader and less steep – between Cley and Blakeney Point.

21

Opposite: **Salthouse – bulldozing the shingle ridge higher as a sea-defence.**

Right: **Pebbles gleam in the spray from breaking waves.**

To see a world in a grain of sand
and a heaven in a wild flower
William Blake

Sand dunes are the wind's sculptures. Their crests are as if the wind passing over the sea remembers the pattern of waves and troughs and then tries to sculpt them in sand.

Crested with silver-grey marram grass rippling in the breeze, dunes are a desert world in miniature. Voluptuous curves and hollows conceal much of beauty: a sun-bleached piece of drift wood, a rabbit's track, a cluster of banded snails on a plant stem, a lizard sunning itself, miniature lichen forests and a world of flowers to which bees and butterflies are drawn across the sands.

22

Right: **Sea holly with early morning dew – Holkham.**

Opposite: **Sand dunes crested with silver marram grass at Burnham Overy.**

Sand dunes are a rare and fragile habitat. In spring and early summer flowers including sea holly, pyramidal orchid, bee orchid, bird's-foot-trefoil, hound's-tongue, sea bindweed and lady's bedstraw colour the dunes and skylarks sing overhead. Oystercatchers and ringed plovers lay well-hidden pebble-patterned eggs on shingle areas within the dunes and among the short rabbit-grazed sward of the older, more stable dunes butterflies – including graylings, common blues and small heaths – can be seen. On the North Norfolk coast dunes occur between Hunstanton and Holme; from Thornham to Brancaster; on Scolt Head Island; at Holkham Bay and on Blakeney Point. The highest dunes are found on Scolt Head Island and at Blakeney Point.

Reeds sigh and sway in the wind and on a few special winter days release their feathery seeds which fill the air like tiny snowflakes. The winter's light can turn each tasselled reed-top silver, or at sunset a whole reedbed can glow pinkish-red. In summer the flat, green acres of swaying reeds hide water rails, reed warblers and coots and perhaps even a bittern or otter secluded among the stems. Overhead marsh harriers drift in the breeze on v-shaped wings. Visit a reedbed on a warm windless May or June dawn to appreciate the sheer volume of birdsong: sedge and reed warblers to the fore accompanied by the bubbling notes of little grebes and the 'pinging' calls of bearded tits.

Large reedbeds are an extremely rare habitat, though narrow strips of reed-fringed dykes and ditches can be found at many sites. The largest coastal reedbeds are at Cley and Titchwell Marshes with smaller areas at Holme, Brancaster, Burnham Overy, Burnham Deepdale, Burnham Norton, Holkham, Wells, Stiffkey, Salthouse and Weybourne. They are an important habitat for wildlife, supporting birds including marsh harriers, bearded tits, water rails, and bitterns. Some have traditionally been managed to produce Norfolk reed for thatching.

Opposite: **Winter blizzard at Cley.**
Left: **Feathery reed tops catch the winter sun.**
Right: **Reed warbler with hungry young.**

There are areas of the North Norfolk foreshore where at low tide the sandflats stretch to the horizon and the sea is only a distant murmur. To walk here is to experience a real sense of solitude and isolation but care is needed. The isolated sandflats below the marshes are safe only if you know the tides, can read the weather and are familiar with tidal creeks which fill with amazing speed cutting off a return to the upper shore. These places are the haunt of cockle and bait diggers with local knowledge passed down the generations of the best areas to reap rich pickings.

Higher up the beach the strandline is beach-combing territory: endlessly fascinating with its razorshells, cockleshells, driftwood, pieces of bladderwrack, mermaids' purses, whelk egg cases, starfish, crab claws and carapaces. These are jumbled together with the jetsam of the human world – plastic detergent bottles from Germany and the Netherlands, pieces of blue and orange polypropylene rope, odd timbers with rusted nails and the inevitable piece of polystyrene packing. A long walk following the strandline, especially in winter, is likely to reveal the remains of seabirds. Sometimes only a bleached skull is left. At other times feathered wings attached to a sternum or quite often whole corpses are found. Guillemots, razorbills, gulls, divers, and sea ducks are the most commonly found. Some of these birds will have died from natural causes but others will show the tell-tale signs of oil smearing their feathers.

Sadly these spills are all too common and sometimes hundreds of birds will be affected. Larger carcasses such as seals or porpoises are also occasionally found. Even large whales have been washed up over the years at several sites along this stretch of coast, most recently at Stiffkey in 2003 and Thornham and the Wash in 2004.

Extensive intertidal sandflats are found in the Wash and at many points along the North Norfolk coast between Holme and Blakeney. Remote sandbars in the Wash and between Morston and Blakeney Point are breeding grounds for colonies of common seals. Good sandy beaches are found at Hunstanton, Holme, Titchwell, Brancaster, Holkham, Wells, Sheringham and Cromer.

Left: **High style on Brancaster beach.**
Right: **Waiting for the storm – Brancaster beach.**
Opposite: **Sunbathers dwarfed by the immensity of sands at Holkham Bay.**

26

Cliffs are an important element of the North Norfolk coastline with outcrops of very different character found at each end of the area. At the western end are the distinctive coloured Hunstanton cliffs. These are formed of three distinct bands of rock. The dark brown carstone, a type of sandstone, forms the bottom layer and then sandwiched between this and the white upper chalk is a metre-thick layer of fossil-rich Hunstanton red rock. The vertical cliffs here are home to a large, noisy colony of fulmars. Rock debris around the base of the cliffs provide a rich area for fossil hunting where belemnites, ammonites and fossil sponges may be found.

At the eastern end of the coast, from Weybourne to Cromer and beyond, are soft cliffs formed from loose sediments of sands, gravels and clays of glacial origin. They reach heights of up to 30 metres between Sheringham and Cromer but, being subject to frequent collapses, are usually steeply-angled rather than vertical. On average the cliffs are eroded a couple of metres a year, a process caused not only by winter storms eating away at the base of the cliffs but also by freshwater seepages and rainfall, resulting in frequent landslips and mudflows depositing material on the beach. Some of the millions of tons of sands and gravels eroded each year on this section of the coast are thought to help replenish and maintain North Norfolk's beaches.

Gaps and low points in these glacial cliffs have influenced the history of the coast, with Sheringham, East and West Runton and Cromer developing at sites where fishing boats could be safely launched from the shore. Equally, for many centuries, gaps in the cliffs were used by smugglers to offload contraband from small boats. Consignments of brandy, tea and tobacco would be quickly loaded into horse-drawn carts on the beaches and moved at night to safe hiding places on secluded heaths, or hidden in local farm houses and inns.

Today the cliffs are much studied for their record of the Ice Age. Areas such as West Runton are famous for the fossils of birds, fish, snakes and mammals found in a deposit at the base of the cliffs known as the Cromer forest bed.

28

Eroding cliffs – West Runton (left), **Weybourne** (right).   Opposite: **Hunstanton cliffs – winter view.**

Dragonflies skim over clear waters on transparent gauze wings, a sedge warbler sings, frogs croak hidden amongst the floating duckweed, a moorhen jerkily makes its way across the water flicking its tail in alarm, while a lone heron stands motionless awaiting its prey. This summer snapshot could be taken on almost any reed-fringed dyke along this coast.

There are no great rivers or extensive lakes in North Norfolk, though the vast estuary of the Wash, which forms the western boundary of the area, depends on the twice-daily mixing of tidal salt water with silt-laden freshwater flowing in from the rivers Great Ouse, Little Ouse, Nene and Welland.

The North Norfolk coast has smaller and more intimate rivers: the Burn, Stiffkey and Glaven, which meander through some of the area's most attractive farmland. Trout and their predators, otter and heron, frequent these rivers

and there are still places where you can lean on ancient stone bridges and watch the sea trout make their way upstream to spawn.

There are reed-fringed freshwater lakes and pools at Holme, Titchwell, Holkham and Weybourne, where reed and sedge warblers, water rails, grebes and the occasional bittern make their homes. However, it is the ditches and dykes forming 'wet fences' on the grazing marshes that provide vital corridors for wetland wildlife to move along. Each dyke is a miniature world, home to countless freshwater minibeasts – food for a lapwing chick, stickleback or even a young grass snake. Sit quietly by one of these dykes and you can be sure of a 'happening'. Water voles and otters, while not easy to observe, sometimes leave signs of their presence. Harvest mice, also secretive, are not uncommon in reeds, rough grass and bramble areas close to the dykes.

31

Opposite: **The river Burn looking north to Burnham Overy mill.**
Above: **Fly fishing for trout – North Norfolk.**

Fields of sugar beet and cereals, cattle and sheep-grazed grasslands, woodlands, hedgerows and lanes, flint-walled barns and farmhouses – all are elements of the North Norfolk farmland mosaic. The farmland adjoining the coast is surprisingly varied, though this landscape has not been immune to the trends affecting the rest of Norfolk. Larger fields, loss of hedgerows and an increase in the proportion of intensively farmed arable land have resulted from the inexorable pressures of agricultural economics. The main crops today are winter wheat, barley and sugar beet, with smaller acreages of potatoes, oil-seed rape, carrots and other vegetables including peas and beans. The coastal saltmarshes are no longer grazed by sheep as they once were but many of the freshwater grazing-marshes, reclaimed from former saltmarsh, still carry livestock, mainly cattle in summer and sheep in winter.

Woodlands and hedgerows have survived because of their game interest. Pheasant and partridge shoots are traditional over the winter period, though many shoots now refrain from shooting woodcock which have declined in breeding numbers.

The farmed hinterland plays a vital part in the ecology of the North Norfolk coast. Huge numbers of pink-footed geese are dependent on the large, open sugar beet fields of north-west Norfolk where they gather in early winter to feed on the sugar beet tops. Lapwing and golden plover flocks are a regular sight on

arable land, actively feeding at night as well as by day. North Norfolk's farmland supports some of the best populations of grey partridge in the UK as well as vast numbers of keepered pheasants. Barn owls hunting along roadsides and field edges remain a familiar sight. Sadly other farmland species, such as yellowhammer,

tree sparrow and corn bunting, are much less common today than in the past. Wheat and barley fields stained red with poppies are now a rare sight in the Cromer to Sheringham 'poppyland' area. Fortunately there still remain many roadside verges where poppies delight the eye with their colour.

Above: **Traditional farmland produce – Little Walsingham. (Sadly this shop is no longer open.)**
Opposite: **Field patterns on the coast at Warham.**

32

Ancient and beautiful, the North Norfolk heaths are special places where there is a powerful sense of the past. Some of the deeply cut lanes and track-ways leading across them are certainly centuries old and may even have been routes walked by the Bronze Age peoples who buried their dead here in mysterious round barrows.

There are secret, secluded places where you can sit surrounded by a golden sea of gorse in early summer, listen to nightingales singing from blackthorn thickets and, as the sun sets, await the 'churring' of nightjars among the scattered birch and pines.

In the past heathland was a vital part of the economies of many coastal villages. These areas were common lands where the poor had grazing rights for geese, horses and sheep. Heathland products included faggots of hot-burning gorse for the baker's oven, bracken collected as bedding for livestock, turves and flags cut for winter fuel and rabbits farmed in warrens for the pot.

More than 90 per cent of the heathland area that once existed in North Norfolk has gone. Enclosed in former centuries, much is now under the plough. Other areas have suffered more recent neglect. Without grazing by sheep, cattle or horses scrub and trees soon take over the open heathland. Today, while they have little economic value, all the remaining heaths are important for their special wildlife. Common lizards, slow worms, adders, rare silver-studded blue butterflies, glow-worms and many unusual plants and birds can still be found. In late summer the combination of purple heathers and yellow gorse, framing views down over coastal villages and across tall-towered churches to the marshes and the shimmering North Sea beyond, is one of the finest sights in North Norfolk.

34

Above: **Superb camouflage – a grayling butterfly on Kelling Heath.**
Opposite: **Salthouse Heath – a patchwork of colours in late summer.**

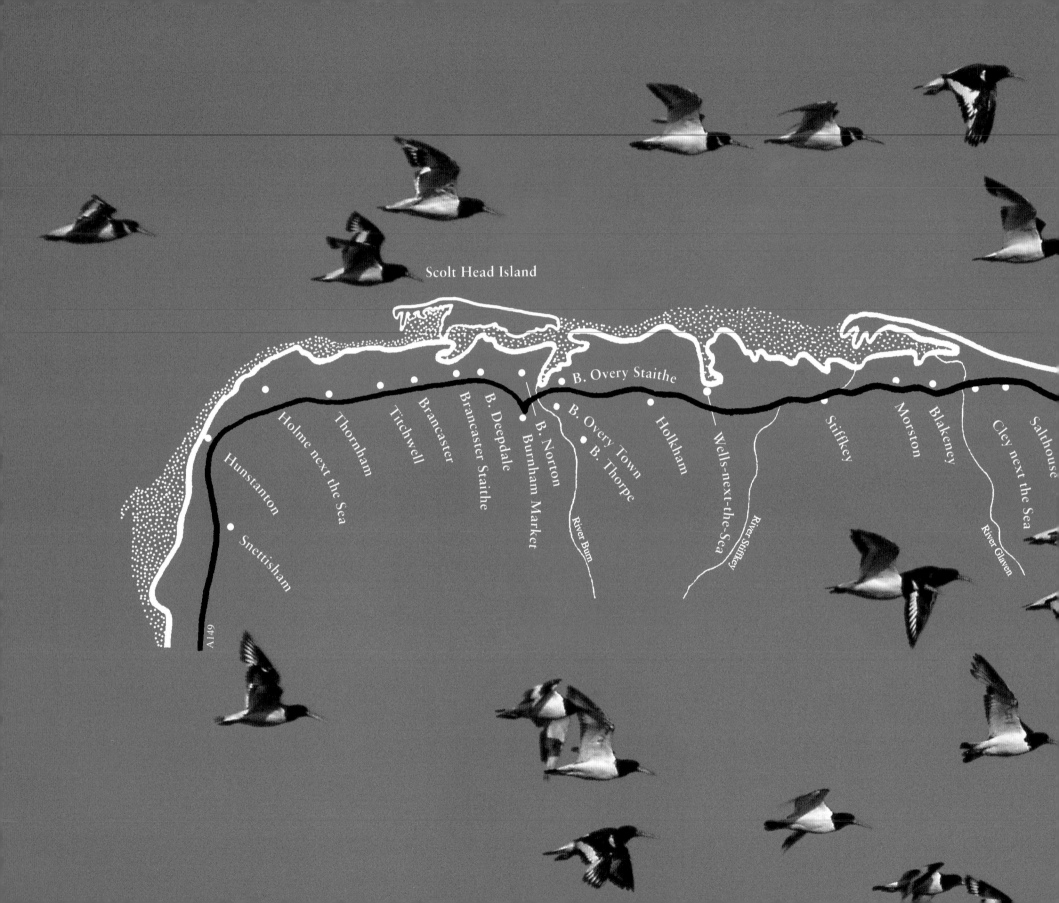

Scolt Head Island

B. Overy Staithe

B. Overy Town

B. Thorpe

B. Norton

Burnham Market

B. Deepdale

Brancaster Staithe

Brancaster

Titchwell

Thornham

Holme next the Sea

Hunstanton

Snettisham

Holkham

Wells-next-the-Sea

Stiffkey

Morston

Blakeney

Cley next the Sea

Salthouse

River Burn

River Stiffkey

River Glaven

A149

Weybourne
Upper Sheringham
Sheringham
West Runton
East Runton
Cromer

GAZETTEER

Cromer crabs
Runton dabs
Beeston babies
Sheringham ladies
Weybourne witches
Cley bitches
Salthouse ditches
Langham fairmaids
Blakeney bulldogs
Morston doddermen
Binham bulls
Stiffkey blues
Wells bitefingers
And the Blakeney people
Stand on the steeple
And crack hazel-nuts
With a five farthing beetle

(Trad.)

SNETTISHAM AND THE WASH

PEOPLE AND PLACE

Opposite: **Sunset over Wash mudflats.**   Above: **Birdwatchers and birds! Snettisham RSPB reserve.**

In summer the Snettisham coast is a magnet for holidaymakers. Its sandy beaches and those of nearby Hunstanton contrast with the muddy shoreline and saltmarshes more typical of the Wash elsewhere. The Snettisham RSPB reserve is also a major attraction for birdwatchers from across the country, especially in autumn and winter. Few of these visitors, whether birdwatchers or beach seekers, visit Snettisham village which lies two miles inland. A history of reclamation of the original marshes, begun in Roman times, has reduced the total area of the Wash by at least a third. Villages like Snettisham, whose communities once made their livelihoods from the marshes and the sea, are now surrounded by farmland. Their residents are more likely to commute to King's Lynn, Norwich, or even London than make their living from the land.

The local building stone, an attractive warm brown sandstone, gives a distinctive appearance to many houses here. Honey-brown carstone has been quarried at Snettisham for nearly 1000 years, and even today a working quarry is close to the village. Snettisham's Rose and Crown pub, a fourteenth century coaching inn and medieval haunt of smugglers, is a fine example of carstone architecture.

Across the main road from the village the approach to Snettisham beach is perhaps not the most scenic in North Norfolk, though the ramshackle collection of holiday chalets and painted wooden huts that back the beach does, in a strange way, have its own distinctive charm. However, the views from the beach across the Wash are memorable. The setting sun reflected on miles of wet mud and sandflats together with the calls of waders flying past make this a wonderful place to simply sit, feel the wind, smell the sea and watch the world turning.

TIME AND TIDE

Smugglers and treasure: the Snettisham village sign depicts both, though the treasure pre-dates the smugglers by more than a thousand years. The Snettisham sign shows a golden torc, two smugglers and a smugglers' square-rigged sailing boat.

The golden torc celebrates the finding of one of the most spectacular archaeological treasures in British history, a find so significant that it puts the small, sleepy village of Snettisham on the national and indeed international archaeological map.

The story of the finding of Snettisham's treasure begins back in 1948 when a local farmer was ploughing his field. He stopped to pick up a curious lump of metal turned up in a furrow but then threw it aside thinking it was just part of an old brass bedstead. It remained lying on the field edge for over a week until a local resident spotted it and thinking it looked interesting took it to Castle Museum in Norwich to be identified. Here its true value was immediately recognised as an outstanding example of a 2000-year-old Iron Age gold torc. Worn around the neck, torcs are thought to have denoted high position and authority and may have been displayed in battle as talismans. There were further discoveries after ploughing in the same field in 1950, 1964, 1968, and 1973, after which it was assumed that nothing more remained. However in 1989 permission was given for metal detecting in the field and on the 25 August 1990 a bronze container filled with scrap metals was unearthed. This interested the British Museum who began serious excavations leading to the finding of five further hoards. The biggest find came on the last day of the dig when, hidden below a hoard of silver and bronze torcs, a larger and deeper pit was discovered. This contained ten exquisite gold torcs as well as more silver torcs and bronze bracelets. In total the finds of torcs, coins and metal ingots weighed

30 kg, much of it in gold and silver. This is the largest find of treasure trove gold in British history and in total, this Snettisham field has revealed 175 torcs: 75 almost complete and fragments of at least 100 more. There are still many unanswered questions about Snettisham's treasure. While originally it was thought items may have been hidden by people fleeing from the Romans, the treasure is now dated around 70 BC, too early for this to be the explanation. The sheer beauty and craftsmanship of these finds, some now on display in the Castle Museum, Norwich, reminds us just how sophisticated and wealthy the residents of Snettisham were, more than 2000 years ago.

Moving to more recent centuries the smugglers' ship on the village sign is there for good reason. The wild marshes fringing the Wash with their winding muddy creeks made them ideal places for landing contraband which was then moved secretly inland. A battle between dragoons and four smugglers took place at Snettisham in July 1737 when seven hundred weight of tea was impounded. Two of the smugglers were escorted to Norwich and jailed in the Castle. Their fate goes unrecorded.

If you visit Snettisham village look out for the old watermill: a lovely carstone building and a fine example community spirit. In 1800 Snettisham villagers got together and raised enough money from within the community to build their own mill so that everyone in the parish could get their grain milled cheaply. Today the community is trying to raise funds to restore the now derelict mill to its former glory.

Above: **Snettisham village sign.**

FLOTSAM AND JETSAM

~ What's in a name? Snettisham, recorded in the Domesday Book as Snetesham, literally means Snet or Snaet's settlement. Who Snaet was and when he lived is lost in the mists of time.

~ Gingerbread houses. The golden honey-coloured houses built from carstone are known locally as 'gingerbread houses'.

~ The great Norfolk goose disaster! On 3 January, 1978 a violent thunder storm crossed the Wash panicking geese from the Snettisham flock into the air. It is thought the birds became caught in a mini tornado 'funnel' cloud and were sucked upwards to high altitude. The result was that dead geese rained down in a 50 km line between Castle Acre and Norwich with at least 140 birds left dead. The Snettisham flock was reduced that day from over 4500 birds to just 640, though most were dispersed by the strong winds not killed.

~ Seal Sands. Remote sand banks out in the Wash are home to the largest breeding colony of common seals in Britain.

~ Continent crossers. More waders have been ringed by the Wash Wader Ringing Group along the shore of the Wash than anywhere else in Britain. Birds ringed here have later been found as far away as Barbados, Yakutsk, Peary Land in Greenland, Ellesmere Island in Canada and South Africa.

~ Fast flyers. Some of the waders found on the Wash cover vast distances amazingly quickly. A dunlin ringed in Finland was caught here 15 days later having travelled a minimum distance of 1576 kms. A knot travelled the 1300 kms from Hungary in ten days and a dunlin took just three days to reach here from Sweden. Another dunlin ringed on the Wash was 1495 kms away in Spain just ten days later.

~ Suburban Snettisham. The first of many madcap schemes for major urban development of the Wash was that of Sir John Rennie in 1839. He advocated creating a new county of 150,000 acres by reclaiming the estuary. In 1965 there was a serious proposal to turn the Wash into a huge freshwater reservoir yielding 620 million gallons a day from a freshwater lake of 80,000 acres. Then in 1968 a civil engineer proposed the world's largest airport and a new town to be created by reclaiming 225 square miles of the Wash. These proposals were not jokes – a £2.5 million feasibility study was carried out on the 1965 reservoir proposal.

~ Snettisham ghosts. The most famous Snettisham ghost is that of Henry Barnard buried at St Mary's church Snettisham. His ghostly apparition appeared to Mrs Godeve in 1893 and she was told to travel to Snettisham from London to receive an important message. On arrival she was allowed to spend a night in St Mary's and is said to have received a message for the Cobb family who owned Snettisham Hall. Nobody has ever divulged what the message was.

41

WILDERNESS AND WILDLIFE

Swept by wind and tide, silvered by the sun,
Smooth or furrowed, wet and glistening,
Mud hides a thousand wings

The Wash is a vast expanse of tidal mud and sand separating north west Norfolk from the Lincolnshire coast. Its sheer scale impresses. When the tide is out a lonely mudscape stretches endlessly to meet the sky. Life here moves to the rhythm of the tides. Visit Snettisham at low tide and the tens of thousands of wildfowl and waders which depend on these productive intertidal mud and sand flats will mysteriously have vanished leaving a bleak, windswept and apparently lifeless vista. As the tide begins to rise, constant movements of small flocks of wading birds – knot, dunlins, oystercatchers, plovers and godwits – hint at the importance of this area for wildlife. The best time to visit is two or three hours before high tide. Between August and April, when the tides are high enough to force birds off their feeding grounds, then Snettisham offers an unparalleled wildlife spectacle. The extraordinary choreography of wader flocks as thousands of birds twist and turn together is amazing to watch. Their calls, and the sound of thousands of wings passing low overhead, as birds move to safe high tide roost sites on the RSPB reserve is unforgettable.

While most visitors to the reserve at Snettisham are primarily attracted by the bird spectacle, the Wash is also of outstanding importance for a whole range of other wildlife. The apparently lifeless mud hides rich pickings of worms and molluscs, every square metre containing thousands of tiny winkles plus cockles, mussels and marine worms. On the remoter sandbanks common seals give birth in midsummer, safely away from the holidaymakers who throng the caravan parks and beaches. The sea walls and shingle areas are excellent for wildflowers – sea holly, yellow horned-poppy, and sea campion among many others. These in turn attract good numbers of butterflies and their seeds in autumn and early winter provide food for linnets, goldfinches, twites and snow buntings.

43

Opposite: **Air show – flocks of knot wheel over the Wash.**
Above: **Yellow horned-poppies flowering on Snettisham beach.**

WILDERNESS AND WILDLIFE

Above: **High tide wader roost** – oystercatchers and knots carpet the shingle at Snettisham RSPB reserve.
Opposite: **Pink-footed geese flying to their night-time roost on the Wash.**

Snettisham RSPB reserve includes important intertidal feeding grounds for waders and wildfowl as well as saltmarsh and shingle habitats and a series of long, narrow gravel pit lakes which parallel the beach. These pits are home to breeding common terns and black-headed gulls in summer and are excellent in winter for wildfowl and grebes. The bird hides at the southern end of the reserve provide sheltered viewing of the high tide wader roost and of birds feeding out in the Wash. In winter large numbers of pink-footed geese roost on the Wash and at dawn and dusk spectacular flights to and from these roosts pass over the reserve.

The Wash is the largest estuary in the UK and its international importance is recognised by its many designations – National Nature Reserve, Site of Special Scientific Interest, Special Protection Area and Ramsar Site among others. Its saltmarshes and mudflats are vital stopovers and wintering grounds for migratory waders and wildfowl from Europe and North America. The large population of common seals is of national importance. Wash tidal areas support commercial cockle, mussel and shrimp fisheries and its shallow waters are vital spawning grounds for fish including cod, plaice and whiting.

HUNSTANTON

PEOPLE AND PLACE

Opposite: **Hustanton town is set well back from the eroding cliffs.**
Far left: **Hunstanton seafront in summer.**
Left: **Traditional Punch and Judy on Hunstanton beach.**

During the holiday season, Hunstanton, or 'Hunston' as the locals call it, can seem like stepping into an entirely different world from the peace and tranquillity that characterises most of the North Norfolk coast. 'Sunny Hunny' is to North Norfolk's wilderness coast what Blackpool is to the wilds of Morecambe Bay, or Great Yarmouth to the south Norfolk coast, though on a smaller and more intimate scale.

On a summer Bank Holiday, Hunstanton positively hums. There's a fun-fair feel to the busy seafront promenade and the larger caravan and chalet parks such as Searles add live bands, discos and cabaret to the Hunstanton holiday experience. Hunstanton's seafront has also become a traditional bikers' rendezvous on summer Sundays, with rows of shiny bikes, chrome gleaming in the sun and leather-clad bikers amiably posing beside them.

The extensive sandy beach, safe shallow waters and beautiful sunsets drew the first Victorian tourists here for sea bathing and promenading, and these are still the major attraction for families with young children today. Where else on the east coast does the sun set over the sea? And no other resort can offer the delights of rock pooling below pink and white 'coconut ice' cliffs. On wet days there's always the Oasis Leisure Centre which provides pools, aqua slides, roller skating and other sports. Further along the seafront the Sea Life Centre offers encounters of the fishy kind with its shark tunnel as well as the added attractions of otters, seals and penguins. When the sun does shine, and it shines a lot in Hunstanton, the two miles of beach has donkey rides, trampolines and a Second World War amphibious landing craft to take you to see seals on sand bars in the Wash. It's often windy here on the edge of the Wash – ideal conditions for kite flying and kite surfing. With so many attractions it's perhaps not surprising that a million people a year are said to visit Hunstanton.

TIME AND TIDE

Long before modern Hunstanton existed, the higher ground here overlooking the productive Wash was an attractive settlement site. In 1970 during road excavation of Oasis Way archaeologists found evidence of late Neolithic or early Bronze Age activity. Flint scrapers, pottery and antler picks dating from 1500 to 2000 BC were among the finds. In 1977 further finds were made nearby dating from the Iron Age.

Saint Edmund, who was crowned King of East Anglia in 856, is said to have landed at Hunstanton in 833 and built a residence on Hunstanton cliffs where he spent two years translating the Psalms into the Saxon language. This may be legend but the archway, from a chapel built in 1272 to commemorate his stay here, still remains on the cliff top at St Edmund's Point.

Much more recent of course is the town of Hunstanton, or New Hunstanton as it was originally known. The town was created to be an exclusive holiday resort for the fashionable Victorian practice of sea bathing. Old Hunstanton was the seat of the Le Strange family who were first granted land in the Hunstanton area around 1100 AD. Hunstanton Hall became their family residence and in 1843 Henry Stapleman le Strange advertised building plots for sale at the 'Sea Bathing Station of St Edmunds'. At this time there was nothing between Old Hunstanton and Heacham apart from the cliff top ruins of St Edmunds chapel.

The first Hunstanton holiday resort building was the New Inn, today's Golden Lion hotel, which opened in 1846. At first development was slow but the coming of the railway link to King's Lynn in 1862 assured the success of the project. Le Strange had planned well and his vision of a triangular-shaped green, lined on two sides with mock Tudor houses with the third side of the triangle being the shore, can still be appreciated today. Many of the new buildings were built with the attractive mellow brown carstone, quarried at Snettisham. This building stone gives a distinctive character to Hunstanton and many of the surrounding villages.

49

Opposite: **Hunstanton green and bandstand.**

Above: **Hunstanton town sign shows St Edmund with the wolf that, according to legend, guarded his body after he was beheaded by the Danes.**

FLOTSAM AND JETSAM

~ The name Hunstanton means Hunston's enclosure. Old Hunstanton is a Saxon settlement listed in the Domesday Book as Hunestonestuna. Modern Hunstanton is known locally as 'Hunston' or affectionately as 'Sunny Hunny'.

~ Taking the waters. In its Victorian days Hunstanton was promoted as a health resort. The waters from the nearby chalybeate spring at Ringstead were said to have healing properties and the bracing sea air to be helpful for rheumatism and anaemia.

~ Something's missing! A traditional British seaside resort should have a pier and Hunstanton used to. The 830 ft pier was built in 1870 but was demolished in 1978 after storm damage in January that year.

~ Smugglers tales. Visit Old Hunstanton churchyard and you will find the graves of two customs officers, William Green and William Webb, killed in a battle with smugglers at Hunstanton in 1784.

~ England's first and largest lavender farm was established near Hunstanton at Caley Mill (Heacham) in 1932 by Linn Chilvers, whose father owned a florist's shop in Hunstanton in the 1890s.

~ The North American princess, Pocahontas, visited the area in 1617. John Rolfe from Heacham village had been exploring North America and was captured by Chief Powhattan. The Chief's 14-year-old daughter begged that his life be spared and he later married the princess. Their visit to Heacham in 1617 is commemorated on the village sign and by a monument in Heacham church.

~ In 1846 when Henry Styleman Le Strange built a hotel at Hunstanton there was no other building between Heacham and the ruins of St Edmunds chapel on the cliffs. The idea was considered so crazy that locals called it 'Le Strange's folly'. The hotel is now called the Golden Lion Hotel and today is at the centre of the thriving town.

~ Hunstanton's cliffs have a long history of cliff falls. One of the largest falls was in 1868 when a cliff fall of about 2000 tons occurred near the lighthouse.

~ In 1900 it took three hours and seven minutes to travel to Liverpool St station from Hunstanton and there were six trains to London a day. By 1922, in the summer months, there were 14 daily trains to London.

~ In 1914 a Zeppelin flew over Hunstanton on the first ever airship raid on the UK. The following year Hunstanton was bombed by another German Zeppelin.

~ The first person to swim the Wash, Miss Mercedes Gleitz, successfully completed the swim in 1929 arriving on Heacham beach. Her civic reception took place in Hunstanton where she had planned to come ashore.

~ The Le Strange family formerly of Hunstanton Hall have traditional rights to the foreshore of Hunstanton. Their hereditary title as Lord High Admiral of the Wash gives them the rights to the shore as far as a man can ride out to sea at low tide and throw a spear.

~ In the floods of 1953 Hunstanton suffered more deaths than elsewhere on the Norfolk coast. There were 31 deaths, including 16 Americans. Without the heroic efforts of American serviceman Reis Leming, who saved 27 lives, the total would have been much worse.

~ Hunstanton's cliff-top lighthouse was used in the First World War as the base for a secret wireless station monitoring German naval signals and in the Second World War as a gunnery and observation station. The lighthouse, built in 1844, is now a holiday home.

Opposite: **After the storm – stranded starfish and razorshells below Hunstanton cliffs.**

WILDERNESS AND WILDLIFE

Along red and white cliffs
stiff-winged fulmars patrol.
They hang, suspended like kites in the wind,
riding the cliff updrafts,
their laughter echoing from carstone and chalk

The cliffs and foreshore at Hunstanton, despite their proximity to the busy coastal resort, are excellent places to view wildlife. The largest colony of fulmars in Norfolk breeds on the cliffs here. At most times of year a walk along the shoreline below the cliffs will guarantee good views of fulmars on cliff ledges. Your attention will be attracted by their raucous 'laughter' with birds being especially noisy between March and May. Fulmars first started to breed here in 1965 and peak summer counts have exceeded 400 birds, though many of these are non-breeders.

At low tide the foreshore below the cliffs is a favourite haunt of turnstones and oystercatchers which pick their way between green, algae-covered boulders looking for food. In winter they are joined by sanderlings, dunlins, ringed plovers and the occasional purple sandpiper.

The 20-metre high cliffs provide a unique vantage point out into the Wash. From the cliff tops, as the tide rises, you can watch small flocks of waders passing by as they move from feeding grounds in the Wash to high tide roosts at Gore Point and Holme. In summer terns plunge-dive for fish in the productive shallow Wash waters. Between August and October they are harassed by skuas, twisting and turning in spectacular aerial chases until the terns disgorge their catch, providing their persecutors with a meal. Sea ducks, grebes, divers and gannets can also be observed from the cliffs. Autumn and winter are the best times and the regular flocks of eiders and scoters reach peak numbers between January and March.

Hunstanton cliffs as well as being visually stunning are a geological Site of Special Scientific Interest (SSSI). Their coloured layers provide a record of deposition in the shallow tropical seas which covered this area between 140 and 65 million years ago. Each centimetre of chalk represents more than 1,000 years of deposition and is formed from the remains of tiny, once-living sea creatures. The jumble of eroded rocks at the foot of the cliffs is good fossil-hunting territory. Belemnites, fossilised shrimp burrows, bivalve shells, sea urchins, ammonites and sharks' teeth can sometimes be found.

Rock pools on the foreshore are excellent places to look for crabs, anemones, shrimps and small fish such as gobies and blennies. This is one of the few locations on the Norfolk coast for rock-pooling.

Opposite: **Fulmars at their nest sites on Hunstanton cliffs.**

HOLME NEXT THE SEA

PEOPLE AND PLACE

The village of Holme, or Holme next the Sea to give it its full title, seems a million miles away from the hustle and bustle of holiday resort Hunstanton, yet lies just a few short miles along the coast road. Holme is even less 'next the sea' than Wells, being separated from the huge and wildly beautiful beaches that form the north-west tip of Norfolk, by over a mile of cattle-grazed fields edged by watery dykes and windswept bushes. North of the village lies the well-known Holme Dunes nature reserve with its reed-fringed lakes. To the west a small road leads down to a public car park with walks across the golf course to Lavender Marsh, the dunes and the sea.

Perhaps because the heart of the village is set back away from the busy coast road, Holme retains a timeless feel of peace and tranquillity. Its fifteenth century church St Mary's, its village pub the White Horse, and the village stores lie hidden from the coast road traffic and the shape and plan of the village seem more aligned to the ancient Peddars Way than to more modern roads. Yes, like other North Norfolk coastal villages Holme has its share of holiday homes and recent incomers, but mysteriously Holme has retained a real sense of community and lost little of its traditional character as it steps into the twenty-first century. This character is reflected in the fascinating range of local building materials used in village houses. Clunch (the local chalk), carstone, flint and locally-made red bricks sometimes feature in a single wall! Look for the various styles of flint used in buildings here, ranging from neat walls of whole cobbles to shiny knapped flints. A Holme speciality is the use of chips of brick and flint embedded in the mortar between larger stones, a technique known as galletting.

Opposite: **The coastline at Holme showing parts of the Norfolk Wildlife Trust's Holme Dunes reserve.**

Above: **A patchwork of chalk, flints and locally-made bricks in a wall at Holme.**

TIME AND TIDE

Holme has at least two claims to archaeological fame. Firstly it lies at one end of a mysterious and ancient route way, the Peddars Way. Secondly in 1998 came a discovery which put Holme at the centre of a major archaeological controversy. The fate of Holme's seahenge, as its Bronze Age timber circle became known, made headlines across the country.

Look at any detailed map of Norfolk and you will have no difficulty in spotting the route of Peddars Way running from the Suffolk border near Thetford to Holme. Most archaeologists recognise this as a Roman route, characteristically straight in many sections, but many also believe it to be much more ancient. Whether pre-Roman Celtic warriors such as the Iceni or even earlier tribes created Peddars Way may never be known. One popular theory is that the Romans used this as a route to a ferry crossing of the Wash creating an important link to the Roman military centres at Lincoln and York. Certainly in medieval times Holme was used as a port. There are records in the thirteenth century referring to a 'keeper of the port of Holme' and in 1326 Holme was asked to supply two ships, each armed with 40 men, for the defence of the realm.

The Romans may or may not have had their Wash 'ferry port' at Holme but Holme's other archaeological mystery predates the Romans here by 2000 years. Holme made the national headlines with the discovery in 1998 of a Bronze Age timber circle on its tidal foreshore. Local media coined the name 'Seahenge' for the discovery and national and international interest was heightened by the huge controversy surrounding the excavation and removal of its ancient timbers by English Heritage in 1999.

The story starts in the early spring of 1998 with the finding of a Bronze Age axe-head on the foreshore by a local worker, John Lorimer, who was going shrimping with a friend. Close to the area of his find John noticed what he took to be a large tree stump sticking roots upward out of the sand. On subsequent visits wooden posts began to emerge and it became clear that these were organised in a rough circle around the stump. By the summer John was convinced, despite others' scepticism, that the feature deserved further investigation and called in expert archaeologists. After initial doubts there was growing excitement that the find was of major significance and this was confirmed in November 1998 when detailed examination of the central stump revealed the presence of tool marks made by bronze axes. Later scientific dating of the wood proved beyond any doubt that this was a Bronze Age monument with 55 timber posts carefully arranged in an ellipse around a central massive block of oak. Incredibly, there were even remains of the honeysuckle rope which had presumably been used to move the timbers.

In 1999, the decision was taken by English Heritage to excavate all the timbers and remove them to Flag Fen in Peterborough for preservation. Despite opposition from both local people and those, including modern-day Druids, who felt this was a site of special spiritual significance, the operation went ahead. For some this was sacrilege and for others simply a way of ensuring that a unique Bronze Age find was not lost to the sea and that its timbers were preserved for future generations to study. It is planned that some, though probably not all, of the find will return to Norfolk for display in King's Lynn museum after the lengthy process of preservation is complete.

Holme's village sign depicts a pedlar, a Roman galley and an oystercatcher – symbols of this area's interest for both human and natural history.

56

FLOTSAM AND JETSAM

~ What's in a name? Holme, spelt Holm at the time of the Domesday Book, most probably means an island in the marshes. There is a Holme in Denmark and it's possible that Holme was named by Danish invaders settling on the coast here. The Peddars Way track may take its name from pedester, the Latin for pedestrian. Others suggest its name is derived from Pedlars Way.

~ A knock down church. Holme's fifteenth century church, St Mary's, is a very unusual shape today. In 1778 the church was considered too big for the village to maintain and so was partially demolished.

~ Changing coastlines. Holme's famous seahenge monument, when it was built more than 4000 years ago, is thought to have been sited on marshy ground between one and three miles from the coastline. Today its site lies on the tidal foreshore.

~ An icy grave. At low tide the wreck of the Vicuna is clearly visible on Holme's foreshore. This ship had been carrying a cargo of ice from Norway to King's Lynn. It sank off Brancaster in March 1883 but the wreck was carried to Holme during storms in 1985.

~ Seahenge – a date with the past. Incredibly, using a combination of different dating techniques, including radio-carbon analysis and dendrochronology, an exact date has been suggested for this Bronze Age monument. It is thought the trees were felled in spring 2050 BC.

~ Seahenge secrets. Seahenge was not really a timber circle. Its timbers are arranged in an ellipse of 18 ft by 15 ft. Marks on its timbers show that at least 38 different axes were used in its construction. These are the oldest metal axe-cuts ever to have been detected in Britain.

~ The *Time Team* at Holme. Channel 4's well-known history programme, presented by Tony Robinson, staged a reconstruction of Seahenge which was broadcast in December 1999. They felled trees with bronze axes, recreated honeysuckle rope and erected an imitation wooden henge at nearby Thornham.

~ The whale's tale. In January 2004 a 60 ft sperm whale was washed ashore at Holme, though later tides moved the carcass to neighbouring Thornham. This is not the first whale to come ashore here. In December 1626 a huge whale was cast ashore at Holme. Accounts from the time describe it as having, '46 teeth, like the tusks of an elephant … the breadth of its tail was 13 feet … the profit made of it was £217 six shillings and seven pence and the charge for cutting it up and managing it £100 or more.'

~ Holme's second Seahenge. While not attracting the blaze of publicity that accompanied the discovery of Holme's first Seahenge monument a second timber ring dating back to 2400 BC was discovered close to the original Seahenge site. Carbon dating has revealed these timbers are also Bronze Age and pre-date the original find by hundreds of years. This second structure is thought to have been part of a burial mound similar to ones known in the Netherlands. Its existence was a well-kept secret until British Archaeology magazine described the find in September 2004. Much of this second circle has already been washed away by the sea during winter storms.

WILDERNESS AND WILDLIFE

Left: **Migratory blackbird feasting on sea-buckthorn berries – Holme Dunes reserve.** Right: **Avocets – courtship display in spring.**

Stormswept wings find rest in an oasis of pine and buckthorn

The shoreline of this north-west corner of Norfolk, where the Wash meets the North Sea, is a remote and magical area. Here sky, sea and land meet, creating ever-changing patterns of light and shade.

Holme Dunes nature reserve, managed by the Norfolk Wildlife Trust, lies right at the point where the North Norfolk coast bends south towards the Wash. It is a wild and varied area including sandy beaches, sand dunes, extensive grazing marshes and a brackish, reed-fringed lagoon, the Broad Water. The isolated group of Corsican Pines growing on the dunes is over 100 years old and creates a prominent landmark visible for miles.

Over 300 species of birds have been recorded in the Holme area which is well known as a migration hot spot. Geographically it is perfectly located both as a first landfall in autumn for birds crossing the North Sea and in spring for migratory birds working their way northwards along the North Norfolk coast. The shelter provided by high dunes, scrub and the isolated group of pines is equally important. The boundaries between the various habitats here seem fluid; sand dunes merging to scrub and grassland, meadows into dyke and reedbed, tidal mudflats into sand and beach. Thickets of sea buckthorn which edge the dunes offer cover for redwings, fieldfares, blackbirds and the occasional ring ouzel in autumn. When the weather conditions are right, 'falls' of migrants can occur in both spring and autumn, often including redstarts,

Left: **Marsh harrier at Norfolk Wildlife Trust's Holme Dunes reserve.**   Right: **Broad-bodied chaser dragonfly (male).**

pied flycatchers, goldcrests, robins and warblers. To the delight of birders these falls sometimes include rarer birds such as shrikes, wrynecks, bluethroats and unusual warblers.

In summer avocets nest here, lapwings cavort over the cattle-grazed meadows and common, little and sandwich terns dive for fish near the sea's edge. Boardwalks cross the extensive dunes which have a rich display of chalk-loving plants. Bee orchids, pyramidal orchids, storksbills, carline thistles, hound's-tongue and bird's-foot-trefoil grow among the short, rabbit-grazed turf. In winter flocks of brent geese and wigeon graze on the inland fields and large flocks of waders frequent the shoreline, especially when spring tides drive them from the Wash.

The importance of Holme Dunes is recognized by its designation as a National Nature Reserve. Norfolk Wildlife Trust owns a 213 hectare reserve here with foreshore, sand dunes, scrub, grazing marshes, freshwater wader scrapes and a brackish reed-fringed lagoon. There is also a smaller reserve and bird observatory managed by the Norfolk Ornithologists' Association.

As well as its considerable bird interest this area is home to a colony of nationally rare natterjack toads. The sand dunes have a rich and varied flora, support a number of unusual insect species, and the dykes and freshwater ponds are rich in dragonflies.

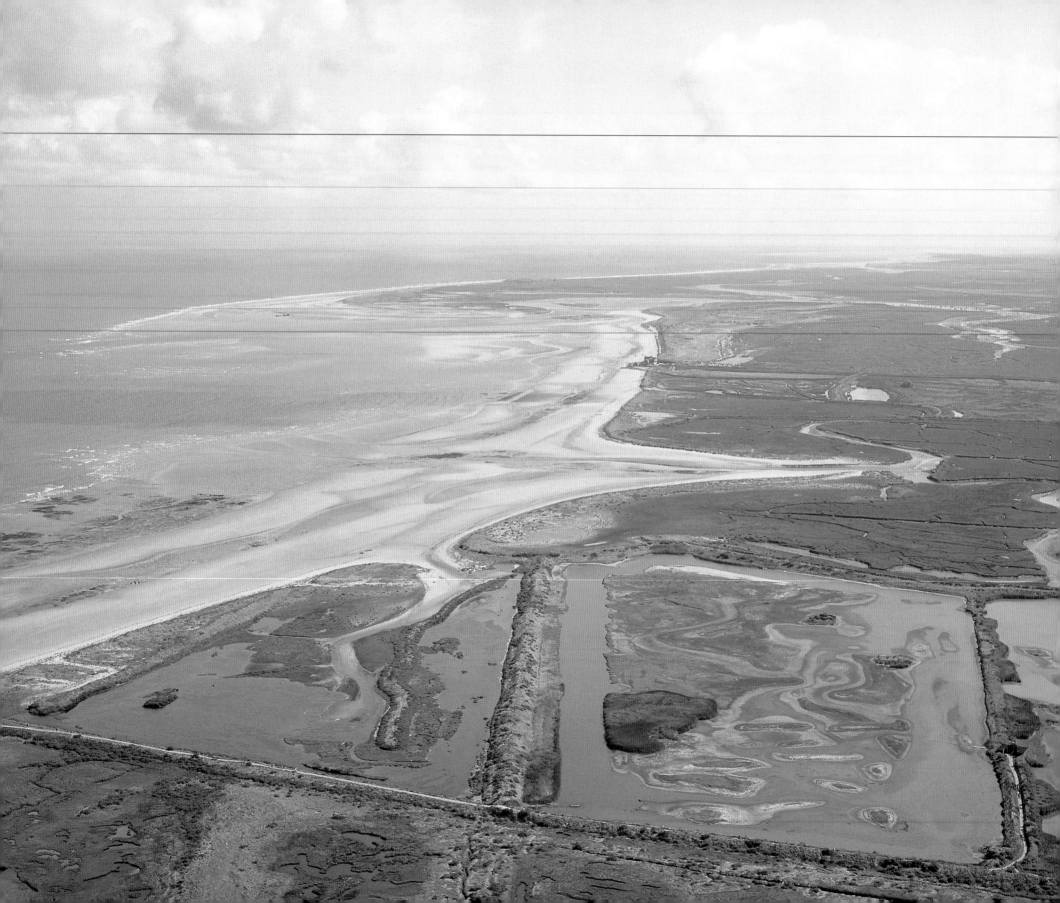

THORNHAM AND TITCHWELL

PEOPLE AND PLACE

Opposite: **The coastline at Titchwell – lagoons at the RSPB reserve in the foreground.**
Above: **Titchwell beach – birdwatchers huddle in the shelter of the dunes.**

Thornham and Titchwell villages lie alongside the coast road and are separated from their foreshores by extensive tidal saltmarshes and reclaimed grazing marshes. Titchwell is probably best known today for its RSPB reserve which attracts over 100,000 visitors a year and doubtless helps sustain the many good B&Bs and hotels found in both Thornham and Titchwell. Its impact on the local economy is clearly significant and aptly summed-up by Steve Rowland, one of the RSPB's Titchwell staff: 'Today in Titchwell there are two places where you can buy a pair of binoculars or telescope costing more than £800, but nowhere in the village where you can buy a pint of milk or a loaf of bread.'

Thornham is the larger of the two villages and boasts three historic pubs, the Kings Head, the Chequers and the Lifeboat. One traditional industry, the farming of oysters in local creeks, has recently been revived. Oysters may have been harvested here since Roman times and today 'Thornham Oysters' market their locally-produced oysters across the UK. Rock oyster seeds are imported from a hatchery in Cumbria and then grown in mesh bags placed on trestles in the tidal creeks. They take several years to reach maturity and are then selected by hand. New European Union regulations mean the oysters must spend a period in tanks ashore. Ultraviolet light treatment is used for purification before they are packed in ice for supply to top hotels across the country.

TIME AND TIDE

Smugglers and wreckers, a medieval trading and fishing port, a Roman fort, a Saxon cemetery and finds of prehistoric flint tools: Thornham and Titchwell between them hold a wealth of historical interest.

The coast at Titchwell is one of the most significant sites in Norfolk for finds of worked flints dating from the end of the ice age some 10,000 years ago. During this Mesolithic period sea levels were much lower than today with the coastline perhaps some 60 to 70 km further away and Norfolk still linked by land to the continent. Evidence that areas now covered by the North Sea were forested in the period after the end of the last Ice Age is clearly revealed by the remnants of tree stumps and woody peat reefs visible on Titchwell's foreshore at low tide. More proof that the coast off Norfolk was once dry land comes from the dredging up, in 1931, of a barbed antler tool dated to around 9800 BC which was found 40 km off the Norfolk coast.

Titchwell was always the smaller of the two settlements. In the Domesday Book Titchwell was a 'beruwic' managed as a small outlier of the wealthy but distant Manor of Southmere. In 1497 this manor fell into the hands of William of Waynflete who gave the land at Titchwell to Magdelene College, Oxford. This Oxford College remained the major Titchwell landowner for several centuries. The fields between the village and the sea have been reclaimed and then flooded again several times during the last 300 years. The land that now includes the RSPB's Titchwell reserve was reclaimed in 1786 by the building of a seawall to enclose the saltmarshes to create new pasture for cattle and as farmland for potatoes. This area remained farmland until the 1953 floods breached the sea wall and the farms were then abandoned allowing marshland to develop. The RSPB, recognising the potential of this area as a nature reserve, purchased the site in 1973.

Thornham also has a wealth of history. In Roman times there was a small coastal fort here, probably an outlier to the main Saxon shore fort at Brancaster. The Romans would have used the creeks at Thornham as

shelter for their square-rigged galleys. Much later, in medieval times, Thornham was a small but thriving sea port with granaries and jetties. Well into the nineteenth century, trading ships were landing cargoes of coal and oil cake here, with malt and grain the main exports. The arrival of the railway at Hunstanton spelt the end of this trade but remarkably a new industry came to prominence in the 1880s. From 1881 Thornham became a centre for iron working and by 1897 there were five blacksmiths employing up to 25 people at forges in the village.

Above: **Thornham and Titchwell village signs – note the anvil and forge on the Thornham sign and the avocet on Titchwell's.**

FLOTSAM AND JETSAM

~ What's in a name? Thornham, recorded as Tornham at the time of the Domesday Book means a settlement with thorn trees. The name Titchwell is derived from a place with springs or a well. At the time of Domesday it was written as Tigeswella.

~ The Thornham forge. Thornham rather surprisingly had a thriving iron-working industry which began in 1881. Work from its foundry was exhibited in Paris and Brussels and it took commissions from King Edward VII. The forge closed in 1920 and was on the present site of Thornham's garage and petrol station.

~ Thornham's truncated tower. The church at Thornham lacks a full tower. It used to have a tall square tower but this collapsed in the seventeenth century.

~ Plague pits. A clump of trees to the west of the road leading down to Thornham harbour is said to be on the site of a plague pit where Thornham's victims of the Black Death were buried.

~ Thornham smugglers. Thornham's creeks were ideal for landing contraband. It was such a notorious smuggling centre that it had its own coastguard centre where excise men were based. The well-known Thornham smuggler William Southgate, locally known as Captain Southgate, died in Norwich Castle prison in the 1780s. In December 1782 excise officers from Wells were attacked by a gang of smugglers at Thornham and tea they had seized earlier was retaken by the smugglers. The small navigable creek that runs through the marshes to the old 'coalhouse' at Thornham was where, in February 1783, excise officers found four hundredweight of tea buried by smugglers in the sand.

~ A barn with Great Expectations. Thornham's well known 'coalhouse' barn is a prominent landmark on the marshes alongside Thornham creek. It featured in the 1999 TV production of Dicken's classic, *Great Expectations*. The barn was transformed for this £3.5 million production into the house and forge where Pip spent his youth.

~ Tanks at Titchwell. During World War II Titchwell Marsh was used as a tank firing range. Remains of concrete bunkers and pill boxes can be seen on the beach and marshes here.

~ Titchwell's ancient forest. Remnants of an ancient forest form a dark reef at low tide on the foreshore. At the end of the last Ice Age sea levels were much lower than today. As the climate warmed, by 8000 years ago, there were forests of oak, alder and elm growing on land now covered by the North Sea. Norfolk was connected to continental Europe and it wasn't until 6000 years ago that the sea level rose submerging and preserving this forest. On the high tide line it's usually possible to find lumps of peat which have eroded from these forest beds and careful examination will reveal the well-preserved remains of twigs, bark and sometimes seeds.

~ Of oysters and oystercatchers. Thornham's creeks still produce oysters. At the time of Dickens there were huge natural oyster beds along the North Norfolk coast and at this time oystercatchers probably lived up to their name and ate them. Oysters may well have been harvested at Thornham in Roman times to supply the centurions at nearby Branodunum coast fort. It is said that the Romans would pay for them by their weight in gold. Even then they were considered an aphrodisiac, perhaps from the Greek myth of Aphrodite, the goddess of love, who emerged out of the sea from a giant oyster shell.

63

WILDERNESS AND WILDLIFE

Reeds whisper tales told to them by the wind
Remembering ancient forests now covered by sea and sand

The combination of a wildly beautiful coastal landscape and a wealth
of wildlife is a powerful mix and perhaps explains why Titchwell is the
RSPB's most visited reserve. The shoreline between Thornham and
Titchwell is backed by huge, open areas of saltmarsh – a true wilderness
much of which is inaccessible.

   If you want space, silence and solitude the small marshland footpaths
north of Thornham village will take you into a world of creeks and sky
where redshanks and curlews call and the wind tastes of salt. For birdlife,
then Titchwell is the place. The wide skies, whispering reeds and windswept
lagoons of the RSPB's reserve throng with birds at all seasons.

   In spring dunlins, sandpipers and plovers urgently probe the mud for
hidden food, 'refuelling' here for journeys which will take some beyond
the Arctic Circle.

   A public footpath runs along a raised embankment to the beach at
Titchwell. From it elegant black and white avocets are easy to observe
in summer. They nested here for the first time in 1984. Titchwell must
also be the best place in North Norfolk to watch marsh harriers drifting
over reeds carrying food to their nestlings.

Opposite: **Thornham creek – the Northern Prince has seen better days!**
Right: **Ancient posts edging Thornham creek.**

Above: **A merlin on a look-out post – between Thornham and Titchwell.**
Opposite: **Bar-tailed godwits landing on Titchwell beach.**

In autumn and winter the reserve's lagoons, carefully managed by dykes and sluices to control both water level and salinity, provide attractive feeding ground for waders. Ruffs, black-tailed godwits, snipe, redshanks, curlews and golden plovers are regulars and between August and October it's not unusual to have more than 20 species of wader here. Among them will be 'Sammy', the reserve's famous black-winged stilt, which has spent the last ten years here.

Winter brings small flocks of twite, snow buntings, and shore larks to the saltings and dunes. The beach is one of the best in Norfolk for large numbers of waders, usually including grey plovers, bar-tailed godwits, sanderlings and oystercatchers. After winter storms it's often covered with shells including mussels, dog whelks, razorshells, piddocks and oysters. These attract huge numbers of gulls to feed. Titchwell ranks as one of the best all year birdwatching sites in Britain.

Most of the coastline between Thornham and Titchwell is natural saltmarsh fronted by tidal sand and mudflats. The area which now forms the RSPB's Titchwell reserve is very different having originally been reclaimed as farmland. The 1953 floods left the farmland derelict and by the time the RSPB purchased the site in 1973 it had already begun to return to tidal saltmarsh. Intensive management by the RSPB has created a series of different habitats here. A walk down the Gipsy Lane footpath between the coast road and the beach is a lesson in ecology, passing alongside scrub, willow carr woodland, reedbeds, a freshwater lagoon, a brackish lagoon, tidal saltings and sand dunes before reaching the beach and foreshore. Around 300 species of birds have been recorded here and important breeding species include avocets, marsh harriers and bearded tits. Other wildlife includes water voles, 17 dragonfly species, 23 butterfly species and rare insects such as the dune tiger beetle.

BRANCASTER, BRANCASTER STAITHE AND SCOLT HEAD ISLAND

PEOPLE AND PLACE

The villages of Brancaster and Brancaster Staithe lie on the 'edgeland' where the wild meets the managed. Seaward are patterned marshes with tangled networks of pools and creeks. Landward the gently rising ground is divided into large, productive fields of wheat and barley. Seen from the air, man's farmland world creates a straight-edged chequerboard landscape so very different from the complex snake-like mazes of curving channels that form nature's marshland. Brancaster has a long, and in winter desolately beautiful, sandy beach backed by a narrow strip of dunes. In contrast, at Brancaster Staithe the foreshore extends as a vast, windswept area of tidal mud and sandflats stretching out to the distant sand hills of Scolt Head Island.

The Staithe is a popular sailing centre, well known for its Sharpies – a class of yacht – and home to a sailing club, chandlery and sailing school. While most of the boats at moorings in the creeks are pleasure craft the Staithe is still a working harbour with whelk sheds and piles of crab and lobster pots. Mussels are farmed near the harbour; seed imported from the Wash takes up to three years to develop on the lays, before being harvested by hand. The sheds contain purification tanks where the mussels are flushed with sterilised water before going for sale. A few boats still land crabs, lobsters and whelks at the Staithe, their arrival announced by the strident calls of waiting gulls. The main street of Brancaster naturally has a splendid seafood shop. Brancaster and Brancaster Staithe have two well-known pubs, the White Horse and the Jolly Sailors which both feature local seafood on their menus. The former is one of the few pubs with splendid views across the marshes, and the latter caters for birders with a rare bird alert pager usually on the bar!

The National Trust has an education and outdoor centre here. The old building, known to locals as Dial House from the sundial on its end wall, has been restored as the Millennium Activity Centre which runs courses including sailing, birdwatching, painting and photography, as well as programmes for school parties. Much of the land here is owned by the National Trust, including most of Scolt Head Island. It is sometimes possible to visit Scolt Head by boat from the Staithe but there is no regular service.

The road from Brancaster village to the beach crosses marshes and reedbeds and ends at a car park by the golf course. The clubhouse of the Royal West Norfolk Golf Club, a distinctive landmark for miles along the coast, now forms a promontory and all that prevents it becoming an island cut off at high tide are the imported boulders acting as its sea defence. Parts of the dunes here have suffered erosion with a number of the golf club's fairways narrower now than in the past!

One end of Brancaster's beach in recent years has become a centre for kite surfing and kite buggying. In summer Brancaster beach is justifiably popular, being one of North Norfolk's best stretches of sand and an excellent location to watch the sunset.

Opposite: **Brancaster Staithe – farmland, village and saltings at low tide.**
Above: **Harvesting mussels at Brancaster Staithe.**

Left: **Fishing boats – Brancaster Staithe at low tide.**   Right: **Sharpie yacht race off Scolt Head Island.**   Far right: **Sharpies off Brancaster.**

TIME AND TIDE

Brancaster's village sign shows the head of a Roman centurion, an appropriate reminder of this area's Roman past. The site of Branodunum, the third century Roman shore fort, now just a grassed field, can be viewed from the coast path east of Brancaster and is clearly marked by a National Trust information board. Little can be seen on the ground but aerial photography has shown that Branodunum was an extensive and important Roman site. There have been several archaeological excavations, the first in 1846 and others more recently in 1974 and 1976, carried out before modern housing was built over part of the Roman vicus (civilian settlement) sited east of the fort. Two beautiful gold Roman rings have been found dating from the period between 270 and 320 AD. It is suggested that the Dalmatian cavalry was based here. This fort was part of a chain of shore forts built to deter the Saxon pirates who regularly attacked merchant shipping and raided East Anglian coastal settlements during the third century AD. In 1960 a Romano-British cemetery was discovered close to Brancaster's church, the skeletons buried east-west indicating that these were Christian burials.

The shape of the coast here has doubtless changed over the centuries but creeks in the area of Brancaster Staithe may well have been used for fishing and shellfish production since Roman times. During the seventeenth and eighteenth centuries the harbour here was also busy with sailing vessels bringing in coal and exporting grain and malt. In 1797 Brancaster Staithe is reputed to have had the largest malthouse in England. This building, like several others in the village, was partly built with Roman stone dug out from the shore fort. It was demolished in 1878.

For most of Brancaster's long and fascinating history fishing and farming have provided the mainstays of local livelihoods, but it's easy to forget that trade and its dark side, smuggling, were also significant for many centuries. As late as the 1830s smuggling vessels were being apprehended off the coast here. A report in November 1832 describes coastguards stationed at Brancaster seizing a boat laden with 5565 lbs of tobacco and 650 gallons of brandy. This contraband was then taken and impounded at the Customs House at Wells.

Above: **Brancaster village sign depicts the head of a Roman centurion.**

FLOTSAM AND JETSAM

~ What's in a name? It has been suggested that the name Brancaster means 'Burnt castle'. More likely is that Caster is derived from the Latin castra meaning a Roman fort and Bran from the Old English for yellow flowered broom. The Domesday Book names this site Broncestra.

~ Peat from the past. At low tide peat beds are revealed in Brancaster harbour and examination of pollen grains preserved in this peat have identified the trees that grew here at a time of much lower sea levels. About 8000 years ago there was woodland here with birch and pine the dominant trees and oak, elm, hazel and lime also present. Other layers of peat in the harbour contain beech pollen. These, only exposed on low tide and sometimes including whole tree stumps, are thought to date from about 2000 years ago.

~ Look Sharp. Brancaster Staithe is the UK centre for the class of sailing boats known as Sharpies. The 40th European Sharpie Championship was held here in July 2003 with 55 Sharpies taking part in the race.

~ The Wreck. Between Brancaster and Scolt Head Island lies the wreck of the Vina, a 1021 ton ship built in 1894 as a cargo vessel. In 1940 she was requisitioned by the military at Yarmouth to be blown up if a German invasion was imminent and used to block the harbour. Fortunately this was never necessary and so in 1943 she was moved to Brancaster for use as a target for planes training for the Normandy invasion. At various times it has been suggested the wreck is a hazard which should be destroyed but local fishermen oppose this as she has become a local aid to navigation!

~ Brancaster's AA box. In a lay-by next to the main A149 coast road, just along from Brancaster Staithe, is one of England's smallest listed buildings. The traditional AA box is more than 30 years old and is now protected as a listed building.

~ Smugglers tales. Dutch smugglers used to anchor their large vessels in Brancaster Bay to sell contraband to small local boats. These large Dutch vessels were heavily-armed with three and six-pounder guns and would be crewed by up to 60 men. They could carry 50 tons of tea and up to 2000 half-ankers of geneva (gin) each trip. The harbour at Brancaster became so notorious for smuggling that in 1710 Customs Commissioners stationed a preventative vessel here.

~ Heated by mud. The National Trust's Millennium Activity Centre at Brancaster Staithe has a pioneering heating system extracting heat using pipes buried in the tidal mud and a heat exchanger. It is one of the greenest buildings in North Norfolk and also makes use of solar energy.

~ D-Day Brancaster. Top-secret documents only revealed in June 2004 show that Brancaster beach was used to plan the Normandy D-Day landings. The beach at Brancaster was selected because of its similarity to Normandy beaches. Trial bombings were carried out at Brancaster in May 1944. These showed that 250 lb bombs would be the most effective. In the actual Normandy landings, based on the Brancaster findings, 523 tons of 250 lb bombs were dropped by 269 aircraft.

73

WILDERNESS AND WILDLIFE

Skeins of geese pattern winter skies
ebbing and flowing like dawn and dusk tides
across boundaries of land, sea and sky

Brancaster has a stern beauty. Its windswept marshes and long sandy beach backed by a narrow dune ridge can seem bleak and desolate on a grey day. At low tide shelducks leave footprint trails across the sand and mudflats between here and Scolt Head and there are almost always redshanks, curlews, bar-tailed godwits and dunlins probing the mud for food. In summer, as the tide creeps in and marshland channels fill, terns call raucously as they swoop and dive for fish.

In winter up to 2000 brent geese frequent this area, grazing the marshes alongside wigeon and teal. At dawn and dusk the flights of pink-footed geese moving from potato, sugar beet and carrot fields inland of Brancaster to their roost on Scolt Head Island is one of the most spectacular of North Norfolk's many wildlife sights. Almost a third of the world population of pink-feet winter along the North Norfolk coast and the traditional Scolt Head roost often exceeds 30,000 birds. In November 2002 68,000 were counted at this roost, the highest number ever recorded at a single site.

Scolt Head Island is one of the remotest parts of the North Norfolk coast. In the summer season there are sometimes boats from Brancaster Staithe and Burnham Overy which take visitors to the island. This service is not regular and depends on the vagaries of weather, tides and the moods of local boatmen. In summer the island has the largest tern colony in North Norfolk. Numbers vary from year to year but often exceed 3000 pairs of sandwich terns plus a few hundred pairs of common terns and smaller numbers of little terns. The breeding area at the western end of the island is strictly wardened with no access to visitors allowed between April and August. However there is much other wildlife interest among the constantly shifting patchwork of Scolt's sand dunes, saltmarshes, shingle ridges and mudflats. The sand dune flowers – sea campions, sea bindweeds, sea hollies, bee and pyramidal

orchids – are a delight in May and June. Any summer walk here will be accompanied by skylarks' songs and the piping of oystercatchers. Like many remote small islands Scolt Head has a special quality of freedom, space and peace.

This area of the North Norfolk coast is protected by the National Trust, Norfolk Wildlife Trust and English Nature. Scolt Head Island was one of the first coastal reserves in Norfolk. All of the island, apart from its eastern end, was purchased by the National Trust in 1923, with the remainder of the island being acquired by Norfolk Wildlife Trust in 1945. Today it is managed by English Nature who lease the island and warden its important tern colonies in spring and summer.

Most of the mainland coastline between Brancaster and Brancaster Staithe is owned by National Trust who purchased the 626 hectares of the Brancaster Manor estate in 1967. This was their first acquisition in Norfolk under the 'Enterprise Neptune' campaign.

As well as extensive saltmarshes, important for wintering wildfowl, the coast here is a breeding area for terns. The large sandwich tern colony on Scolt Head supports up to 25 per cent of the UK breeding population. The island is also an important traditional winter roost site for tens of thousands of pink-footed geese. The sand dunes on Scolt Head are some of the highest in North Norfolk and support an interesting flora including several orchid species.

Opposite: **Pink-feet silhouetted against a fiery sky – Brancaster**
Above: **Bar-tailed godwits in the snow – Brancaster Staithe**

THE BURNHAMS

PEOPLE AND PLACE

The group of villages known collectively as the Burnhams are scattered either side of the river Burn in some of the most attractive countryside in North Norfolk. The largest and best known is Burnham Market, which has a delightful spacious tree-shaded green at its centre and is lined on either side by gracious Georgian houses. Known as Little London or Chelsea-on-Sea because of the influx of wealthy 'furriners' since the 1970s, this is prime second home country – at least if you have several hundred thousand pounds to spare – and many former visitors have chosen to retire here. This influx of wealth has brought changes, good and bad. You will find two nationally acclaimed restaurants here. The Hoste Arms and Fishes Restaurant are only a few buildings apart and face the green on Burnham Market's main street. For a village of its size the range of top notch food and wine shops is remarkable as well as others selling stylish clothes, antiques, books and jewellery. The green here is a lively cosmopolitan place in summer and especially busy in July and August when the carnival, flower show and a popular craft fair take place.

Few visitors to Burnham Market will take time to explore the other six Burnhams. Furthest west lies Burnham Deepdale with a winding creek connecting it to Brancaster Staithe, wonderful marsh walks along its sea walls, and a classic North Norfolk round-towered flint church. Also fringing the marshes are Burnham Norton and Burnham Overy Staithe. The Staithe is a popular spot for sailing at the mouth of the river Burn and at low tide the channel is a wonderful area for paddling, crabbing and generally having fun in the water. Inland and easternmost

is Burnham Thorpe, famed as the birthplace of Nelson, with a fine church and a pub – named The Nelson of course. Both these buildings are a treasure trove of Nelson memorabilia.

The final two Burnhams are Burnham Overy Town (a small village!) and Burnham Westgate, the latter really the western end of Burnham Market.

Opposite: **Burnham Market busy during its annual summer craft fair.**
Above: **Burnham Deepdale's popular jazz festival.**

TIME AND TIDE

London, York, and Coventry
And the seven Burnhams by the Sea
(Trad.)

The importance of this area in medieval times is illustrated by this old traditional verse. Burnham Market held a market charter in 1209, earlier than any other North Norfolk settlement, apart from Wells.

The river Burn, like the Stiffkey and Glaven further east, was originally tidal for many miles inland. Prior to the 1400s it was tidal as far inland as North Creake but around 1400 it is recorded, 'sea gone back and river embanked'. These changes may in part have been a result of natural silting causing changes to the river estuary. At one time the Burn flowed out to sea at Burnham Deepdale but as Scolt Head Island grew, the river mouth was deflected eastwards.

The wealth of the Burnhams was based on sheep. Overy means a sheep farm and the ancient drove road, shown on today's OS map as Gong Lane, runs straight from Overy Town to the marshes which provided summer grazing at Overy Staithe. In the early 1300s grazing land was taxed in wool. Most of East Anglia paid one wool sack for each 1500 acres but in North Norfolk it was a sack for every 600 acres reflecting the wealth of the area. The other source of wealth was malting barley. The former large maltings at Burnham Overy Staithe were converted into the well known Moorings Hotel which closed in the early 1970s.

Even in the space of two generations huge changes have affected the

Burnhams. Gone are the days when most people living here would have been born within walking distance of the house where they spent their adult lives. Only 50 years ago Burnham Market had a cattle market every Monday. Today this is a predominantly arable landscape. Fifty years ago you could catch a train from Burnham Market to Wells, Norwich, Heacham or even a through train to London. Then there were five pubs in Burnham Market, of which only two, the Hoste Arms and the Lord Nelson now remain. In the 1930s and early 1940s horses still ploughed the fields, there was no mains electricity and paraffin lamps lit the village houses. At this time there were three bakeries, a foundry, a shoemaker, a blacksmith's forge, a saddler and a harness maker trading in Burnham Market. The 1920s and 1930s were tough times in North Norfolk with people finding work where they could – buying and selling wild rabbit skins being one way of making a living.

All this has changed, and in most ways for the better. It's a romantic illusion to think that life was anything but hard then. The days when most people worked in agriculture and a single farm could field a cricket team with its labourers belong to a very different but not so distant era. Today tourism and commuting sustain the wealth of the Burnhams with only a handful of villagers making a living directly from the land or sea.

Above: **Village sign – Burnham Thorpe birthplace of Nelson.**

78

FLOTSAM AND JETSAM

~ What's in a name? Burnham means a settlement by a river. Burn is derived from the Old English Burna for a stream or river. In the Domesday record it was written as Bruneham.

~ Birthplace of Nelson. Horatio Nelson was born on 29 September 1758 in the rectory of All Saint's church, Burnham Thorpe. He was the son of Edmund Nelson the parson. Though the rectory building no longer exists a plaque on the wall close to the church marks the site of his birthplace.

~ Famous timbers. The wood of the cross and lectern in Burnham Thorpe's church is made of wood from Nelson's ship *HMS Victory*.

~ Anyone for tea? Richard Woodget, born in the Burnhams, became captain of the famous tea clipper *Cutty Sark*. During his time as captain he broke many trans-Atlantic speed records. He retired to Burnham Overy and lived in the property now named Flagstaff House on the shore line at Burnham Overy Staithe between 1899 and 1926. He died in 1928 and is buried in Burnham Norton churchyard.

~ Horatio Lord Nelson specified in his will that he wanted to be buried at All Saints church Burnham Thorpe, 'unless the King decrees otherwise'. The King, George 111, did decree otherwise and Nelson was buried in St Paul's Cathedral.

~ At the Nelson pub in Burnham Thorpe you can drink in the room where Nelson once gave a party for the villagers before leaving Burnham Thorpe to captain the Royal Navy ship the Agamemnon.

~ The disappearing Goosebeck. A stream named the Goosebeck sometimes flows through the centre of Burnham Market creating a ford across the main street. In some years it flows for nine months and in other years for as little as six weeks. The water originates from a chalk aquifer and arises as a spring situated west of Whiteway Road. This flows into the 'Fishpool' at Burnham Westgate before being channelled as the Goosebeck through the centre of Burnham Market.

~ Burnham Market was originally made up from three smaller settlements, Burnham Westgate, Burnham Sutton and Burnham Ulph. Ulph was a Danish Chieftain and the brother of King Canute.

~ Burnham rice paddies. Sequences from the James Bond film, *Die Another Day*, were filmed at Burnham Deepdale. Flooded grazing land was converted into a landscape of rice paddies for the film. The closing sequences of a helicopter flying over rice paddies into which two sports cars have fallen was shot here.

WILDERNESS AND WILDLIFE

Redshank's warning, curlew's call
Silence permeating every sound

The coastline between Burnham Deepdale, Burnham Norton and Burnham Overy Staithe is comparatively sheltered and extensive saltmarshes have developed in the lee of Scolt Head Island. Reclaimed by centuries-old sea walls, freshwater marshes also form a wonderful wildlife habitat in their own right. In spring lapwings tumble in spectacular courtship displays over cattle-grazed pastures, redshanks call in flight or stand alert on wooden fence posts, and marsh harriers patrol in search of unwary prey. The dykes – wet 'fences' which separate one block of grazing from the next – are home to grass snakes, dragonflies and frogs. Herons stand hunched in field corners, or wait poised for prey on dyke edges and in the reeds which fringe these dykes, reed and sedge warblers sing to establish territories or busily seek food for hungry young.

In winter, from November to March, the grazing marshes are alive with large flocks of brent geese and wigeon and the edges of shallow pools within the fields are favoured by teal, snipe and redshanks.

For an unparalleled experience of this environment follow the Norfolk Coast Path from Burnham Deepdale around to Burnham Overy Staithe. The path follows the top of a seawall and offers contrasting views. On the seaward side lie saltmarshes and to landward the freshwater pasture of Deepdale and Norton Marshes.

There is a very different walk, but one of my personal favourites, from the car park at Burnham Overy Staithe to the sand dunes of Gun Hill. From the Staithe follow the sea wall. This is a superb vantage point for birdwatching with views over the estuary of the river Burn. From the harbour to the sea is roughly two kilometres of fairly easy walking, though in winter the path can be muddy and slippery. At low tide Overy Creek always has a good selection of waders feeding on its muddy winding channel. Dunlins, redshanks, curlews, grey plovers, oystercatchers and ringed plovers are joined at migration times by godwits, sandpipers, greenshanks and stints. There are nearly always shelducks here and as the tide moves in and the channel deepens, look for sleek cormorants diving for fish. The marram-covered dunes and the fine sandy beach reached by a boardwalk at the end of the seawall form a pleasing contrast to the earlier parts of this walk. Between April and June the dune slacks have wonderful displays of marsh and pyramidal orchids and, with luck and keen eyes, you may also spot bee orchids. By late June and July rosebay willowherb colours the sides of the dunes in fiery pink drifts and the yellow ragwort is being munched by large numbers of black and orange cinnabar moth caterpillars which strip the plants, leaving only a spiky stem behind. Even in winter this walk is a delight, with brent geese, pink-footed geese and wigeon often in large numbers on the fields which back the dunes between here and Holkham.

Above: **Brent geese flying low into the wind – Burnham Overy marshes.**
Opposite: **Burnham Overy Staithe – looking seawards to the mouth of the River Burn.**

WILDERNESS AND WILDLIFE

Another favourite Burnham haunt is the old water mill, now owned by the National Trust and converted into holiday flats, which lies on a sharp bend of the coast road between Burnham Overy Staithe and Burnham Norton. Lean on the old stone bridge which crosses the river Burn here and very often there are sea-trout lying in the pool below. Otters use this stretch of the river and there are usually swans, little grebes and wagtails to watch. The fields next to the coast road just beyond the bridge are prime barn owl hunting territory and it's often worth pausing here in late afternoon to enjoy the spectacle of a barn owl methodically quartering the ground in search of prey.

The North Norfolk coast between Burnham Norton and Burnham Overy Staithe forms part of the huge Holkham National Nature Reserve (NNR). Holkham NNR was established in 1967 and, covering around 4000 hectares, is one of the largest NNRs in England. The saltmarshes and freshwater grazing marshes of the Burnhams are also protected as part of the North Norfolk coast Site of Special Scientific Interest (SSSI). This area of the coast is internationally important for the numbers of brent geese, pink-footed geese and wigeon that winter here. Deepdale Marsh, Norton Marsh and Overy Marsh together form the largest area of freshwater grazing marsh on the North Norfolk coast. Significant for wintering wildfowl they are also important breeding areas for redshanks and lapwings. Reedbeds at Burnham Deepdale, Burnham Norton and Burnham Overy provide breeding habitat for bearded tits and marsh harriers, and wintering grounds for bitterns.

83

Top: **Sea rocket carpets the upper foreshore at Burnham Overy.**
Bottom left: **Bee orchid – Burnham Overy dunes.**
Bottom right: **Sand dunes – Burnham Overy.**
Opposite: **Barn owl at Burnham Norton on a frosty winter morning.**

HOLKHAM

PEOPLE AND PLACE

Holkham, a tiny village and a huge estate, lies at the heart of the North Norfolk coast roughly midway between Hunstanton and Cromer. The village is a cluster of well-kept, pretty Victorian cottages at the northern entrance to Holkham estate. It has fewer than 200 inhabitants and is really part of the estate with most of the people living here employed at Holkham and many families having lived here for several generations. The estate is vast, over 3000 acres, and surrounded by a brick wall nearly nine miles in length. The park which has an attractive lake, some wonderful trees and a large herd of fallow deer is open to the public, as is the impressive though austere-looking Holkham Hall. The Hall is the best example of Palladian architecture in Britain and has a sumptuous collection of rare paintings, sculptures and fine art. Attractions for visitors include the Holkham Pottery, Bygones Collection and the walled garden centre. Adjacent to the coast road is the Victoria Hotel which provides good food, a warm welcome and a much-appreciated haven especially after an icy winter's walk in the park or along the shore.

There is something magical about the coast at Holkham. Despite its popularity with visitors it still retains a quality of timelessness and tranquillity. Even on summer weekends, when Lady Ann's Drive, the access point to the beach, is crowded with cars and thronged with holidaymakers this remains true. People come to Holkham to walk their dogs, to fly kites on the beach, sunbathe in the dunes, walk through the pines, to birdwatch or to visit Holkham Hall and its many attractions. This is a place of recreation in the true sense of the word. A place to breathe deep, slow down and allow the Holkham atmosphere to 're-create' you, at least sufficiently to return to the busy madness of the twenty-first century refreshed and renewed. What is it that gives Holkham this special quality? Perhaps it's the sheer sense of space and freedom. At low tide the sea seems to retreat to the horizon though its presence is still there in the low murmur of distant waves. The huge, sweeping expanse of beach at Holkham Bay runs for miles and, backed with fragrant pines, on a warm summer's day has an almost Mediterranean feel. It's a place to wander barefoot, to pick up shells or marvel at the haze of sea lavender that colours the marshes purple in late summer. In winter racehorses from Newmarket are brought here to exercise when the Newmarket gallops are frozen hard. Mounted soldiers from the Household Cavalry also come each summer and gallop their horses through the surf. There is a biannual Holkham Fair which attracts thousands to Holkham Park for the displays of countryside crafts and produce. Whatever the season, Holkham is one of the best places to discover the special nature of the North Norfolk coast and be captivated by its magic.

Opposite: **The wild beauty of Holkham Bay.**
Above: **The Household Cavalry exercise their horses on Holkham Bay.**
Overleaf left: **Holkham Bay framed by dark pines.**
Overleaf right: **Holkham Hall and Park busy at the biannual Holkham Fair.**

TIME AND TIDE

There was a settlement at Holkham more than 1000 years before the Earls of Leicester created the Holkham Estate. The earthworks of an Iron Age fort are still visible on the marshes at Holkham and date from around AD47. This was an Iceni settlement, the tribe famed for fighting the Romans under their Queen Boudica. Is it romantic to think that Boudica herself or her daughter may have come here?

In Roman times foot soldiers would have tramped the route that now forms the western boundary of Holkham Estate, perhaps travelling to or from the shore fort at Brancaster. On the OS map the route of this Roman road, running south from Holkham to Toftrees, is easy to follow.

Holkham also has associations with Anna, King of the Angles in the seventh century AD. Anna may have lived here for a period and the Church of St Withburga, which stands on a Saxon mound within the Holkham estate, is named after one of his four daughters who died in AD 743 and was revered as a saint.

The Vikings are thought to have sailed their longboats up tidal creeks at Holkham and to have established a fort on the marshes here in the ninth or tenth century AD.

The view in medieval times would have been quite different from the present one. The high tide line would have been roughly where the main coast road is today and Holkham Staithe was a small but busy harbour capable of holding fishing boats and trading ships of some size. There were no pines on the sand-dunes then and where there are grazing marshes today lay tidal creeks and saltmarsh. By the 1500's the channels had silted considerably but smaller fishing vessels still used the Staithe and the site of the present-day Holkham lake was still linked to the sea as a tidal creek.

The more recent history of Holkham is inseparable from the story of the Coke family. Present day Holkham Hall was the vision of Thomas Coke, who began building in 1734. He inherited the Holkham Estate lands in 1707 when he was only ten and at the age of 15 embarked on his six-year Grand Tour of Europe which so influenced his later vision for Holkham. During his time in Italy he developed a passion for the classical style of the Renaissance architect Andrea Palladio. By the time he

returned to England he needed a large house to display the amazing collection of classical treasures he had amassed. The creation of Holkham Hall and its landscaped grounds involved the wholesale removal of at least one village, explaining the now isolated church within the park.

Thomas died before his vision for the Hall was complete but the work continued under his nephew Thomas William Roberts who inherited the estate in 1776 and took the family name. It was this Thomas that became known as Coke of Norfolk and pioneered new agricultural systems at Holkham which influenced farming across England. Coke's 'Norfolk four course' replaced the previous system of leaving fields fallow every third year and he introduced a Dutch system of planting wheat, barley and turnips in succession, using a crop of clover to replace nitrogen in the soil and provide winter grazing for cattle.

Coke of Norfolk became the first Earl of Leicester and was also created a peer by Queen Victoria in recognition of his contribution to agriculture. It is said that when he inherited Holkham in 1776 the estate was 'a barren sandy heath of windy slopes where rabbits fought for grass' and by the time he died in 1842 the estate was one of the most efficient and productive in England. His annual sheep shearings, held in the Great Barn, were visited by thousands.

His son, yet another Thomas, was also a pioneer and his planting of the pines on the dunes at Holkham between 1853 and 1891 is said to be the first large scale attempt to stabilise sand dunes in Britain.

Today the estate is still owned by the Coke family. Their landholdings extend far beyond the confines of the original Holkham Estate wall, with much of the coast between Burnham Overy Staithe and Stiffkey included. Most of this coastal area is now managed for wildlife conservation.

89

Opposite: **Holkham Park – a seated bronze statue of Thomas Coke, Earl of Leicester, surveys the deer park and Hall.**

FLOTSAM AND JETSAM

~ What's in a name? The name Holkham may have Viking origins and is said to be derived from the Danish for 'ship town'. It is mentioned in the Domesday Book as Holcham. Another possibility is that it means a settlement in a hollow, from the Old English holc (hollow) and ham (a homestead).

~ Garden make-over. The gardens at Holkham Hall were designed by Britain's most famous landscape architect, Lancelot 'Capability' Brown.

~ Lost commons and displaced villages. Estates such as Holkham grew at least in part at the expense of 'commoners'. In 1794 Norfolk had 143,000 acres of common land and by 1844 only 27,000 remained. The development of Holkham Hall and Park displaced an entire village.

~ Can't see the trees for the wood. The planting of a continuous belt of woodland around Holkham Park was begun in 1780. Over the next ten years it is estimated that 1,057,940 trees were planted.

~ Royalty at Holkham. For many years the Royal family have owned a wooden beach hut or chalet secluded in the pines of Holkham Meals. It was used by the Queen Mother and other members of the Royal family as a base for leisurely afternoon picnics and walks along the beach. Sadly it was burnt down by vandals in 2003.

~ Birthday suits instead of bathing suits. There are eleven officially designated naturist beaches around the British coastline, and the western end of Holkham beach is the only place in Norfolk where it's legal to walk 'sky clad' through the waves. On hot summer weekends hundreds of people travel to Holkham to enjoy an all-over tan and the open beach is dotted with colourful wind breaks where families enjoy this freedom.

~ Filmset Holkham. The wild setting of Holkham beach has proved attractive to film makers over many years. Perhaps the best known film clip featuring Holkham is the closing scene of *Shakespeare in Love* when Gwyneth Paltrow walks across Holkham's sands. Scenes from *The Eagle has Landed* were also filmed here.

~ Ten million bricks. The brick wall surrounding Holkham deer park and Estate runs continuously for about nine miles. It is estimated that more than ten million bricks were used to build it, a task which began in 1833 and took six years to complete.

~ From Italian acorns. The evergreen holm oaks common at Holkham are thought to originate from Italy. It is said that the acorns from which the trees descend arrived mixed in with holm oak leaves used as packing for the valuables that Thomas Coke brought back from his Grand Tour between 1712 and 1718.

~ Taxidermy and twitchers. Long before the advent of modern field guides and optics, the Victorian naturalist was more likely to have carried a gun than a telescope. Holkham Hall holds an amazing collection of stuffed birds: more than 200 species, most of which were obtained locally, are on display at Holkham Hall.

Opposite: **A fox crossing the dunes at Holkham.**

Above left: **Large numbers of wigeon winter at Holkham.**

Below left: **White-fronted geese in the fields next to Lady Ann's Drive.**

Right: **Snow buntings on the foreshore at Holkham Bay.**

Opposite: **Pink-footed geese in early morning mist – fields inland of Holkham.**

WELLS-NEXT-THE-SEA

PEOPLE AND PLACE

Opposite: **Wells-next-the Sea** – the town, harbour channel and saltmarsh backed by farmland.
Left: **Wells** – pinewoods, beach huts and its long sandy beach curving into Holkham Bay.

From Wells quay a wonderful panorama spreads out before you. This is the North Norfolk marshland coast at its best; better than any painting, this living view changes constantly with the tides, the play of light and the seasons. The main harbour channel, a wide stretch of water at high tide, becomes a narrow, meandering, shallow creek at low water.

Commercial trade through the port of Wells is a thing of the past. Most of the small boats, bobbing at their moorings at high water or leaning at crazy angles perched on the sands at low tide, are pleasure boats. The fishing fleet is now reduced to 14 boats which work the waters up to 35 miles out from Wells. The profits today are mainly in crab and lobster, though depending on the season, whelks, shrimps and skate are also taken. Even though tourism has supplanted trade and fishing as Wells' main industry, its commercial history is writ large in its legacy of buildings. Favor Parker's granary (now flats) which closed in 1990 dominates the harbour front and there are many old maltings, now converted to other uses, in the town.

Throughout the summer season Wells is a bustling seaside resort. The narrow main street, Staithe Street, runs up from the quay and is lined with shops and several cafes. Not far from the top of Staithe Street and close to the parish church of St Nicholas, is a spacious green known as the Buttlands. This was once the centre of Wells and its open space provides a site for carnivals and fetes and is fringed by attractive Georgian houses.

Wells is 'next-the-sea' but it's quite a distance to the beach. You can travel the mile to the pine woods, sandy beach and boating lake by road or by narrow gauge train, though by far the best way is to enjoy the walk along the sea wall embankment which leads from the quay to the lifeboat station.

Wells is famous for its whelks and if you explore the eastern end of the harbour you will find the whelk sheds. There were more whelks landed at Wells than any other UK port up to the mid 1990s but, perhaps because of over-fishing, the industry has declined.

TIME AND TIDE

Wells has been a market town and fishing port since at least the thirteenth century. Its market charter dates from 1202. The original centre of Wells would have been near the parish church, appropriately named St Nicholas, after the patron saint of fishermen. Originally there was a tidal channel near the church providing good shelter for small boats, but this was cut off by an embankment built in 1719.

Wells is the closest port to Walsingham, which became a nationally important pilgrimage centre in medieval times. Its attractions included three curative wells, milk of the Virgin Mary, a finger-joint of St Peter and the famed 'Holy House'. The latter was built in the late eleventh century, inspired by a vision of the Virgin Mary and designed as a replica of the house in which Jesus spent his childhood at Nazareth. The popularity of pilgrimages may in part be explained by the medieval belief that going on pilgrimage lessened time spent in purgatory! The Shrine of the Virgin Mary at Walsingham was visited by many of the rich and famous including the scholar Erasmus, Catherine of Aragon and Henry VIII. Did any of these notables arrive by sea at Wells?

The port was busy from medieval times up to the 1800s exporting grain (especially barley), salt fish and malt and importing coal, salt and domestic goods. Wells' fishing boats worked the waters off Scotland, Norway and Iceland and on these long voyages fish such as cod were salted at sea. Apart from fishing the other major industry in Wells was malt production. This reached a peak in the mid 1700s with Wells the second largest producer in the country, with many large maltings at work in the town. To give some idea of the scale of trade, in the mid 1700s grain exports averaged 10,000 tonnes a year and between 1819 and 1822, 11,800 tonnes were exported annually. The importing of coal stopped abruptly with the arrival of the railway from Fakenham in 1852 as it was cheaper to move coal by train.

The port had mixed fortunes in the twentieth century. There were a few good years in the 1930s exporting sugar beet for the Yorkshire Sugar Company, and then an astonishing upturn between 1970 and 1988 when up to 250 small diesel coasters brought in animal feeds, soya beans, and fertilizer totalling up to 100,000 tonnes a year. This trade finally died because newer, larger vessels operating with the same sized crews were far more economic using the larger King's Lynn and Yarmouth ports.

Today Wells can still boast the only safe harbour for large ships on the North Norfolk coast but its visitors today are more likely to be pleasure boats than trading vessels.

Opposite: *The Albatros* at anchor in Wells channel.
Above: **Wells town sign shows a fishing boat, the beach and pines.**

FLOTSAM AND JETSAM

~ What's in a name? Wells of course is named from its wells. The town is built above layers of chalk and many houses had wells sunk to good freshwater aquifers within the chalk.

~ Bite fingers and wreckers. In early medieval times the men of Wells had a reputation for plundering shipwrecks. They earnt the nickname 'bite fingers' from their alleged method of removing rings from dead mariners on the wrecks.

~ The Golden Fleece. Between 1850 and 1880 Wells is reputed to have had 40 public houses. There are not so many today but one of the most historic pubs is the Golden Fleece, on the quayside. Its name is a reminder of the days when the wool trade was a source of wealth for Wells.

~ A horse-drawn lifeboat. The first lifeboat station in Wells was established on the quay in 1868. At low tide the boat had to be pulled by horses down the mile long harbour channel before it reached the sea! The shallow waters had other perils and in October 1880 the lifeboat *Eliza Adams* overturned. Her mast stuck in the sands holding the boat upside down and eleven crew members were drowned.

~ Stranded ships. In the floods of January 1953 the motor torpedo boat *Terra Nova* was lifted onto the quay and left high and dry when the tide receded. More recently, in 1978, a 500-ton coaster was stranded on the quay during storm conditions. The heights of these exceptional storm tides are marked on buildings opposite the quayside.

~ Mutiny on the Bounty. John Fryer who was master of *HMS Bounty*, of mutiny fame, was born in Wells in 1754. He is buried in Wells churchyard and his gravestone can be seen in the church porch.

~ Narrow gauge Wells. Wells is unique in having two narrow gauge railways. The first is the harbour railway built in 1858 and the second, the Wells and Walsingham Light Railway, only opened in 1982. With a track 10.25 inches wide it is said to be the narrowest railway in the world operating a public service. The four-mile track is also the longest 10.25-inch-guage railway in the world.

~ *The Albatros* at Wells. This elegant sailing vessel, a familiar sight in Wells harbour, was built in Rotterdam in 1899. During the Second World War she helped Jewish refugees escape from Germany and shipped arms to the Danish resistance. In the 1990s she worked as a commercial vessel carrying soya beans from Belgium to Wells. More recently she was chartered by Greenpeace to be used in their education work and today she is used as a sail training boat.

~ Early morning archery. The origin of the open space in Wells known as the Buttlands goes back to the time of Henry VIII when this was the site of the town's butts – a space where every able-bodied man was required to practice with the longbow. As Henry's edict has never been repealed, the men of Wells should still assemble on the Buttlands for archery practice each morning in case they are called upon to defend the realm.

Opposite: **Little Walsingham looking north to the sea. From medieval times Walsingham has been an important pilgrimage site.**

WILDERNESS AND WILDLIFE

Sand and sky, wave and cloud
Patterns of movement and stillness

The view from Wells' quay is of a vast, flat expanse of saltmarsh extending like a patterned carpet to the horizon. These marshes stretch north from Wells for more than two kilometres – the widest extent of saltmarshes on the North Norfolk coast. The only landmarks to break their table-top flatness are the two groups of pines on the remote East Hills which somehow only seem to emphasise the sheer scale of this marshland world. This beautiful but treacherous tidal maze is best viewed from a distance as incoming tides and mud like glue make this a dangerous area to explore on foot. The wildlife here can be viewed in safety from the coast path skirting the upper edge of the marshes. This runs east from Wells to Warham Greens and beyond. Skylarks, redshanks and shelducks are noticeable at all seasons and in winter brent geese add their calls to those of waders on the marshes.

At Wells it's not really even necessary to leave the town to enjoy a wildlife spectacle. The quayside provides an excellent observation point in all seasons. In spring and summer black-headed gulls noisily patrol the harbour on the lookout for scraps. Their breeding colony, home to several thousand pairs, can be seen on the marshes in the middle distance. Records suggest a colony has been here for over 100 years. In winter, groups of brent geese come to the harbour channel to bathe, and often graze the nearby football ground and pitch and putt course in dense, dark flocks. Little grebes and cormorants are also regulars in the harbour channel and sometimes, especially in winter, kingfishers use a handy mooring rope as a convenient look-out point.

The mile-long walk along the raised sea bank to the brightly painted lifeboat station, provides opportunities to look for redshanks, turnstones, godwits, dunlins, oystercatchers and ringed plovers which regularly feed along the edge of the channel here. Colourful shelducks dabble in the mud at low tide while curlews call noisily overhead.

Far Left: **Pyramidal orchid flowering in June – sand dunes at Wells.**
Middle: **Marsh fritillary orchid at Wells Dell – June.**
Left: **Marsh orchid at Wells Dell – June.**
Opposite: **Black-headed gulls over Wells harbour.**

WILDERNESS AND WILDLIFE

Beyond the lifeboat station lie Wells woods. The pine trees here extend along the dune ridge to Holkham. On the landward side of the pines is one of the most famous birdwatching spots in England. Wells Dell is an area of birch, oak and willow scrub which has established itself in the shelter of the pines. Many rare birds have been recorded here. In autumn, fine weather over Scandinavia encourages birds to depart south on migratory flights, but if these birds meet fog and drizzle over the North Sea they will drift on easterly winds to the nearest landfall offering cover and shelter. When these 'fall' conditions occur then every bush in Wells Dell will be alive with warblers, robins, blackbirds, redstarts and flycatchers. Sometimes among these will be rarities such as bluethroats, arctic warblers, red-breasted flycatchers or barred warblers to the delight of the birdwatchers who gather here.

This area inland of the pines is interesting at all times of year. In spring there are wonderful displays of orchids near the boating lake. The tangled scrub of privet, rose-briar, bramble and young trees is good for warblers. Lesser-whitethroats, willow warblers, sedge warblers and garden warblers nest here. In summer and autumn this sheltered area is excellent for butterflies and dragonflies. Commas, red admirals, painted ladies and peacock butterflies find both bramble flowers and later the ripe fruits of blackberries irresistible.

The extensive saltmarshes to the north and east of Wells town are, because of their size and lack of disturbance, among the best in the whole of Europe. Wells Salt Marsh, Lodge Marsh and Warham Salt Marshes cover an area of more than four square kilometres. Beyond them, at low water, stretches the vast remote area of tidal sandflats known as Bob Hall Sand. Saltmarshes usually develop behind the shelter of a dune or shingle ridge as has occurred at Scolt Head Island and Blakeney Point. The saltmarshes north of Wells are unusual in having no such protective barrier. Remote sand banks in this area provide nest sites for little terns and are a long-established winter roost site for up to 25,000 pink-footed geese.

Opposite: **Brent geese flying over Wells channel – the pines of East Hills are in the background.**

Right: **A male kestrel feeds on a chaffinch on a gate post at Wells.**

STIFFKEY AND MORSTON

PEOPLE AND PLACE

Opposite: **Stiffkey marshes looking east to Morston.**
Left: **Seal trip boats on their way back to Morston quay from Blakeney Point.**

Alongside the coast road between Wells and Blakeney lie first Stiffkey and then Morston, two small but very attractive flint villages backed by extensive saltmarshes which have developed in the shelter of Blakeney Point.

Stiffkey is probably best known for its 'Stewkey blues', said to be the tastiest cockles found anywhere along the coast. The houses here line both sides of the narrow main road which twists and turns through the village. The road is extremely narrow here; bordered with high flint walls and with no footpath, there is barely room for two cars to pass. As well as the village stores there is a well-known lamp shop and an excellent and historic pub, the Red Lion. The village lies in the shelter of the valley of the River Stiffkey and it's well worth exploring the lanes and footpaths inland of the coast road. There are still traditional water meadows grazed by cattle here – a rare sight in Norfolk today.

Morston is the smaller of the two villages. Many visitors come here to catch the seal trip boats operating from Morston quay. The quay and the marshes between here and Blakeney Point are owned by the National Trust. The Trust's look-out tower near the quay provides excellent views over the marshes to Blakeney Point and to the east you can see the twin towers of Blakeney church. There are paths across the marshes with rickety plank bridges crossing deep muddy gulleys and, along the main creek, spindly-looking landing platforms provide access to boats from mid tide onwards. There are still a few crab and lobster fishermen working out of Morston and commercial mussel beds are worked in the tidal areas between here and Blakeney. Morston's one pub, the Anchor, is a good traditional 'local' and has been owned by the Temple family, who now run some of the seal trip boats, for over 100 years. Given its location it's perhaps not surprising that this pub is well-known for its fish and shellfish menu.

TIME AND TIDE

Stiffkey has always been a larger and historically more important settlement than neighbouring Morston because of its location on a tidal estuary. Today the river Stiffkey flows almost unobserved through double sluice gates tucked under the sea wall to enter the tidal waters of Fresher's Creek. However, until late medieval times, Stiffkey village overlooked a magnificent estuary with its river tidal as far upstream as Warham.

At Warham, Iron Age tribal peoples built an impressive fort in a commanding position next to the river Stiffkey. Its double ring ditches are still impressive after the erosion of more than two thousand years of wind and rain. The fort is thought to have been built in the immediate centuries before the Roman invasion.

Stiffkey and Morston were both thriving settlements before the time of Domesday. The extensive coastal marshes provided people with wildfowl, shellfish and samphire. There was fishing in waters sheltered by Blakeney Point and winding creeks provided access to the sea for trade. Stiffkey gained a market charter in 1271 and both settlements were at their medieval heyday by the early 1400s. The light, easily worked, though not very fertile soil, on the rising ground above the villages was classic 'sheep-corn' country. Large open fields were divided into strips with sheep folded onto the land in winter to increase soil fertility and moved down ancient drove ways onto the marshes for the summer. These drove roads are still clearly marked on the OS map with names such as Garden Drove, Cocklestrand Drove, Green Way and Hollow Lane. Stiffkey marshes alone had up to 600 sheep in the sixteenth century. As well as farming and fishing, the inhabitants of Morston and Stiffkey made their livings from spinning wool, tanning, preparing malt from locally grown barley, making butter and cheese and brewing beer. Villages were much more self-sufficient than today. Pigs, chickens, ducks and of course horses for ploughing were familiar parts of the local village scene.

There were big changes to the farmland here between 1793 and 1815 with the majority of the open fields being enclosed by Parliamentary Act. Some idea of the scale of this change is shown at Stiffkey where more than 75 per cent of lands in the parish were enclosed at this time with only parts of the marshes remaining as common land. Many of today's hedgerows, or at least those that have survived the post 1945 trend to larger fields, date from the time of these enclosures.

Opposite: **Gathering samphire on the marshes between Stiffkey and Morston.**
Above: **Stiffkey's sign depicts a common tern.**

FLOTSAM AND JETSAM

~ What's in a name? The name Stiffkey, recorded in the Domesday Book as Stivecai, is said to mean island of tree stumps. This could perhaps relate to the remains of tree stumps sometimes uncovered on the marshes. These date from the period more than 8000 years ago when the sea level was much lower and the present North Sea area was a forested land-link to the continent. The origin of the name Morston is much simpler. It means a settlement on the marsh and at the time of Domesday was written as Merstuna.

~ Stiffkey's sex scandal. Stiffkey gained national notoriety when its Rector, the Reverend Harold Davison, was defrocked in 1932 for alleged immoral practices with London prostitutes. Originally commended by the Bishop of London for his missionary trips from Stiffkey to work among prostitutes in Soho, it seems this popular minister's missionary position may not have been exactly what the Bishop had in mind. His undoing came through a compromising photo and the testimony of a working girl, Miss Barbara Harris. Harold Davison protested his innocence throughout his life which sadly came to an end after he was mauled by a lion in the travelling circus he was working for.

~ A whale of a problem. The 60 ft sperm whale which was washed up dead on the shore below Stiffkey marshes in April 2003 became a considerable visitor attraction. Sadly, trophy hunters sawed off its teeth preventing experts from the Natural History Museum using them to study the whale. The carcass provoked considerable argument over who was responsible for its disposal. Under normal circumstances this would be the Receiver of Wreck but if the body rests on privately owned land then it becomes the landowner's responsibility.

~ Thunderbolts and the Second Coming. Morston's parish church, All Saints, was struck by lightning in 1743. The inhabitants believed so strongly in the imminence of Christ's Second Coming that they didn't want to waste their resources on repairing the tower. Some years later, as Christ had not reappeared, a rather hasty repair with bricks was made to the flint tower. This can still be seen today.

~ Marsh trolls, sprites and ghosts. Stiffkey's marshes are said to be haunted by a 'screaming cockler' – the ghost of an unfortunate woman trapped by the tide while gathering cockles. There are many tales of supernatural beings – trolls and marsh sprites – haunting the marshes at Stiffkey and Morston. Doubtless these stories proved useful to the smugglers who really did haunt the remote marsh creeks where contraband was landed.

~ Tarka the Otter and Stiffkey. Henry Williamson, famous for his best-seller *Tarka the Otter*, lived for a decade at Old Hall Farm, Stiffkey. His book, *The Story of a Norfolk Farm*, was published in 1941. In the book he gives the fictional name 'Whelk next to the Sea' to Wells. Descriptions of Stiffkey's characters and local events abound in the book. The house on Stiffkey's main street, where Williamson once lived, is marked with a blue plaque.

~ Stiffkey saffron. An unusual local crop in the seventeenth century was saffron, and Stiffkey Hall in 1636 had kilns and chambers for drying the spice. This valuable crop sold for up to two shillings an ounce.

Opposite: **Warham Iron Age fort – view looking north to the coast.**

WILDERNESS AND WILDLIFE

Marshland patterned in greys, greens and browns
Reflecting boundaries between land, sea and sky

Between Stiffkey and Morston the saltmarshes which begin at Wells continue in an unbroken strip. There are several access points from both villages linking to the long distance coastal footpath. Some of these routes between the villages and the marsh follow ancient green lanes, once used as drove ways. However, by far the most popular access point to the coastline here is the National Trust car park at Morston quay.

The walk in either direction between Morston and Stiffkey offers wonderful views across ancient saltmarshes. This open landscape of ever-changing light and skies has its own special charm. In July and August large areas of these marshes turn a wonderful purple-mauve with carpets of sea lavender as far as the eye can see. Plants with evocative names – seablite, thrift, arrowgrass, purslane and samphire – grow here, each favouring a different level of the marsh. Samphire, a strange cactus-like succulent, favours muddy areas at the lowest levels of the marsh. The best locations for it, on remote mudflats along the seaward edge of the marsh, are well-kept secrets as this local delicacy is still gathered here for sale.

In winter the marshes between Stiffkey and Morston are a prime area for birds of prey. Hen harriers, merlins and peregrines are regularly recorded here and a winter visit in the hours before sunset offers a good chance of spotting harriers drifting over the marshes on their way to night time roosts. Little egrets are also an increasingly common sight here.

In spring and autumn, the narrow belt of trees which edges the inland side of the coast path, separating the marshland world from its farmland hinterland, is excellent for migrant birds. Ring ouzels and black redstarts are regularly recorded at these times and hoopoes, wrynecks and yellow-browed warblers have also occurred here.

The farmland between Stiffkey and Morston, bordering the marshes, is excellent for hares, partridges and barn owls. All three species move between the marshes and the fields depending on conditions and the time of year. The river Stiffkey is a haunt of both otters and kingfishers. Further upstream the cattle-grazed ramparts of Warham Camp have an interesting chalk flora. This peaceful and attractive site is also good for butterflies, including small coppers and common blues.

The saltmarsh coast at Stiffkey and Morston is an ancient landscape with areas of saltmarsh here thought to have formed more than 6000 years ago. The constantly shifting blend of marsh, creek, mud and sand is a true wilderness. The saltmarshes act as a natural sea defence, trapping silt with every tide that covers them, and gradually building to higher levels. In places more than eight metres of sediments have collected keeping pace with rising sea levels over their long history.

Between Wells and Blakeney lie over 1000 hectares of saltmarshes – one of the best and least spoilt areas of this habitat in Europe. Morston and Stiffkey Marshes are owned and protected by the National Trust. Both areas were purchased as part of the National Trust's Enterprise Neptune campaign – Morston Marshes in 1973 and Stiffkey Marshes in 1976.

Opposite: **Sea lavender colours the marshes at Morston.**
Above: **July and early August are the best months to enjoy sea lavender in full flower.**
Overleaf left: **Peregrine falcon feeding on a teal – Morston marshes.**
Overleaf right: **Sperm whale carcass – Stiffkey sands, April 2003.**

III

Above: **Rescue** – taken to a sea bird sanctuary this oiled guillemot was later released back to the wild.

It's not unusual to find the remains of dead birds along the shoreline. Most often the bodies lie among the tangle of seaweeds, shells and odds and ends of human junk that mark out the lines of recent high tides. Some of these birds are likely to be victims of North Sea oil pollution whereas others will have died of natural causes. Major oil spills are fortunately rare but the regular but insidious pollution caused by even small leakages of oil means that frequently the corpses show the tell-tale stains of oil on their feathers. Some oil is said still to leak from ships sunk as long ago as the Second World War. However natural seabird 'wrecks' can also occur and numbers of dead seabirds wash ashore after severe weather. In March 2004 a large wreck of seabirds occurred along the North Norfolk coast with several hundred dead fulmars as well as other species including guillemots and sea-ducks involved.

Less frequently the remains of seals or even dolphins and porpoises are washed up on the shore. In many of these cases it's difficult or impossible to tell if the cause of death is natural or man-made.

Above: A dead guillemot on the tide-line – Morston.

Above right: Oil spill victim – a stranded guillemot.

Below right: The remains of a long dead seal – Morston.

BLAKENEY AND BLAKENEY POINT
PEOPLE AND PLACE

*Believe me, my young friend, there is nothing – absolutely nothing – half
so much worth doing as simply messing about in boats*
Ratty from *Wind in the Willows* by Kenneth Grahame

Blakeney can boast the only harbour still open on the Glaven estuary,
and its sheltered waters, protected by Blakeney Point, make this the
sailing centre of North Norfolk. On summer weekends, as the tide rises,
dozens of brightly coloured sailing dinghies and yachts tack up the
narrow Blakeney channel to the more open waters of Blakeney Pit.
On some days, particularly when the high tide falls at a convenient
daytime hour, the water off Blakeney becomes a Piccadilly Circus for
yachts. It's amazing that more collisions don't occur!

Blakeney High Street has a charm all of its own. It slopes steeply
down to the quay and its pubs, shops and cafes are a popular spot for
visitors. Narrow alleyways known as 'lokes' lead off the High Street into
yards, some formerly used for shipbuilding or as coal and grain stores.
A chandlery and marine stores on the quayside service Blakeney's sailing
industry and the Blakeney Hotel, a fine spot for morning coffee or lunch,
has commanding views over the saltmarshes across to Blakeney Point.

Exploring Blakeney on foot, look out for the flood markers which
show the levels of the storm surge tides in 1897, 1953 and 1978. A
public barometer near the bottom of the High Street was once crucial for
fishermen to judge whether to set sail. A rapidly falling glass might mean
a decision to retire to one of the many local pubs. Sadly, the Crown and
Anchor, known to locals as the 'Barking Dickey', popular with fishermen,
and in former centuries with smugglers, was demolished in 1921.

Opposite: **Piccadilly Circus for yachts – Blakeney harbour on a summer weekend.**
Above right: **Having fun at the regatta – the greasy pole competition.**
Below right: **The annual tug of war across Blakeney channel.**

117

TIME AND TIDE

Boat building, fishing and trading: it's difficult to imagine just how busy Blakeney port was in medieval times. The original settlement here was known as Snitterley and undoubtedly fishing was its raison d'etre. As early as 1222 there was a fish market and by the 1350s there are records of a great fish fair held annually selling cod, herring, ling and even sturgeon. Harvesting cockles and samphire from the marshes, sail-making, salt and smoked fish production, collecting oysters and mussels, sheep-grazing and rabbit-snaring were traditional ways people made their livelihoods.

However, the real wealth of Blakeney grew with its export trade. By the fourteenth and fifteenth centuries, corn, wool and goods such as malt were being traded with North Sea ports in Belgium, Holland and Norway. Ships up to 100 tonnes could sail from Blakeney and Wiveton harbours up to the sixteenth century until reclamation of neighbouring marshes caused silting and shallowing of the main sea channel. The scale of Blakeney's parish church, St Nicholas, reflects the wealth generated through this trade.

There is a long tradition of boat building in Blakeney and neighbouring Wiveton. As recently as the 1840s ships of up to 80 tons were constructed in Blakeney. The *Hull Packet*, launched in September 1844, was the last of the large ships built here but the tradition just about survives. Traditional wooden fishing boats are still build by David Hewitt at Saxlingham Road and Stratton Long Marine operates both boat repair and construction, building the modern day fibre-glass equivalents of the traditional local fishing boats.

Trading and commercial deep sea fishing out of Blakeney quay are alas no more. The last vessel to trade abroad was in 1889 importing timber from Sweden. However, well into the twentieth century, cargoes of corn, coal, cattle food and fertilizer were unloaded at the quay. Imagine the clatter of horses' shoes on the cobbles as horse-drawn wagons and carts dispersed the goods to yards, warehouses and granaries off the High Street.

Opposite: **Blakeney in its setting – a late summer view.**
Below: **Blakeney's village sign reflects its history of fishing and trading – the fiddler and his dog and the beetle hammers, which feature in traditional stories about Blakeney, also appear on the sign.**

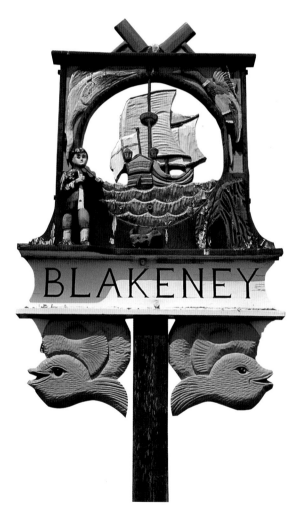

FLOTSAM AND JETSAM

~ What's in a name? At the time of the Domesday Book (1086) Blakeney was called Esnuterle and this name is later recorded as Snuterlea and Snitterley. The name Blakeney was first used in the twelfth or thirteenth centuries and probably means 'Black Island'.

~ The Blakeney fiddler. The story of the Blakeney fiddler and his dog is commemorated on Blakeney's village sign. Legend has it that a fiddler and his dog entered a mysterious tunnel leading from near Blakeney Guildhall. The fiddler's music grew fainter and fainter and he and his dog were never seen again. Rumours of a network of smugglers' tunnels under Blakeney have always been rife. Who knows? One day they may still be discovered.

~ Shiver my timbers. The roofs of some of the older houses in Blakeney are constructed from timbers left over from ships built in the village. These oak timbers were first soaked in sea water for a year to prevent rot and woodworm.

~ The Blakeney Undercroft. This brick-vaulted chamber, owned by English Heritage and open to visitors, is said at one time to have been part of Blakeney's Guildhall. While its fourteenth century origins are still argued about, in more recent times it's been used as a grain store, a coal bunker, a worm and bait store, for growing mushrooms and as a mortuary for bodies washed ashore during the war years. The attractive brick arches are made from Flemish bricks which were used as ballast on the return voyage by Blakeney trading ships sailing back from Holland.

~ Blakeney's church lighthouse. The parish church, St Nicholas, has a curious second tower. This is said to have been used as a lighthouse with its light visible from over 20 miles out to sea.

~ Cart races. When there were granaries off Blakeney High Street the custom was to race the loaded wagons down its slope to the quay. Their momentum was sufficient for them to hit a barrier at the quayside tipping their loads into the holds of waiting ships.

~ I see him here, I see him there ... Baroness Orczy, author of the *Scarlet Pimpernel* books, stayed in Blakeney and was so inspired by local tales of smuggling and piracy that she named her fictional hero of the series, Sir Percy Blakeney.

~ Norfolk's first nature reserve. The National Trust acquired Blakeney Point in 1912 to safeguard the breeding seabirds and protect its unique landscape. This was Norfolk's first public nature reserve.

~ The moving finger ... Blakeney Point has for centuries been on the move, a constantly shifting pattern of shingle, sand-bars, dunes and marsh sculpted by wave and storm. The Point is the western end of a shingle spit running 15.5 kilometres from the cliffs at Weybourne and estimated to contain 82.5 million cubic feet of shingle. Blakeney Point has slowly been extending westwards and at the same time moving landwards as storm-driven pebbles are thrown from the seaward side covering marshes on the inland side. A bird's-eye view of the Point reveals a series of landward curved shingle ridges, like teeth on a comb, each indicating a former end to Blakeney Point. Today the shingle continues to move landwards on average a metre every year and the tip of Blakeney Point is still growing westwards.

Opposite: **Blakeney channel leading out to the open sea beyond Blakeney Point.**

WILDERNESS AND WILDLIFE

Gulls hang on the wind above waves that surge and roar
Beyond a line of shingle
Vast space, an emptiness
Water, sky and silence

Beyond the busyness of Blakeney's harbour lies a world of windswept marsh and mudflat protected from the open sea by the pebble, shingle and sand barrier of Blakeney Point. One of North Norfolk's most celebrated nature reserves, Blakeney Point, is a wild and remote place of solitude, isolation and moody open skies. Its creeks are edged with grey-green purslane and its saltings turn purple with sea lavender in July and August. The plant life here is extremely varied with different species colonising the shingle, sand dunes and saltmarsh habitats. Yellow horned-poppy, sea campion, stonecrop and thrift are attractive flowers characteristic of the shingle ridge. The marshes in contrast are carpeted with aster, purslane, sea lavender and samphire. A dark green jungle of shrubby seablite bushes dominates the upper edge of the marshes in the zone where mud meets shingle. Blakeney's high sand dunes are crested with silver-grey marram grass. Within the sheltered hollows of older dunes, areas are carpeted with grey lichens and a rich flora has developed. May and June are the best months to enjoy a profusion of dune flowers – ragwort, sea holly, sea bindweed, bird's-foot trefoil and orchids.

The Point is better known for its birds than its flowers. In Victorian times this area was recognised as an excellent site to find rare migrant birds in spring and autumn. The motto of these early ornithologists was, 'What's hit is history, and what's missed is mystery', and a gun was considered every bit as important as a glass (telescope). Some of the rarities shot on the Point in the late nineteenth century feature in the taxidermy collections of Holkham Hall, Sheringham Hall and Castle Museum, Norwich. There are bluethroats, wrynecks, hoopoes and sadly even a white-tailed eagle from this period. When easterly winds blow in spring and autumn the Point continues to be an excellent spot to seek wind-drifted rarities. Today's birdwatchers, fortunately for the birds,

123

come armed only with field guides, high power optics and digi-cams to record their finds.

In conservation terms it is Blakeney Point's breeding birds which are of special importance. Four species of terns: common, arctic, sandwich and little, nest on the shingle here. The breeding colony is roped off with access prohibited between April and August, but good views can be obtained from hides provided by the National Trust.

Rabbits, hares, stoats, weasels, shrews, voles and foxes make their home on the Point, but the best known mammals, the ones which attract thousands of visitors, are the seals. Several hundred common seals and smaller numbers of grey seals breed on sandbanks off the Point. From their once remote hauling-out areas, the seals have become accustomed to boats full of staring people, and simply stare back or idly wave a flipper at boats only a few metres away.

Opposite: **Common seals at rest on sand banks off Blakeney.**
Above: **Migratory terns return to nest on Blakeney Point each summer.**

WILDERNESS AND WILDLIFE

124

Blakeney Point was purchased by Charles Rothschild and given to the National Trust in 1912. It was the first public nature reserve in Norfolk and one of the first reserves in England. Today it is still managed and wardened by the National Trust and is now designated as a National Nature Reserve and also protected as part of the North Norfolk coast Site of Special Scientific Interest.

The Point is simply the end of the shingle ridge which extends westwards from Weybourne. The shape of the Point is constantly changing through storms, winds and tides. Over several centuries its length has gradually increased westwards and the shingle ridge has moved slowly landwards. Much scientific work has been carried out here on coastal landforms and ecology. London University have carried out research here since the early 1900s.

In summer the breeding numbers of sandwich and little terns are of national importance and oystercatchers, ringed plovers, redshanks, and shelducks also nest in good numbers. In winter the coastal mudflats and saltmarshes which have developed in the shelter of the Point are important feeding areas for geese, waders and wildfowl.

Left: Sea kale growing on the shingle of Blakeney Point.
Opposite: Seals on patterned sands – Blakeney.

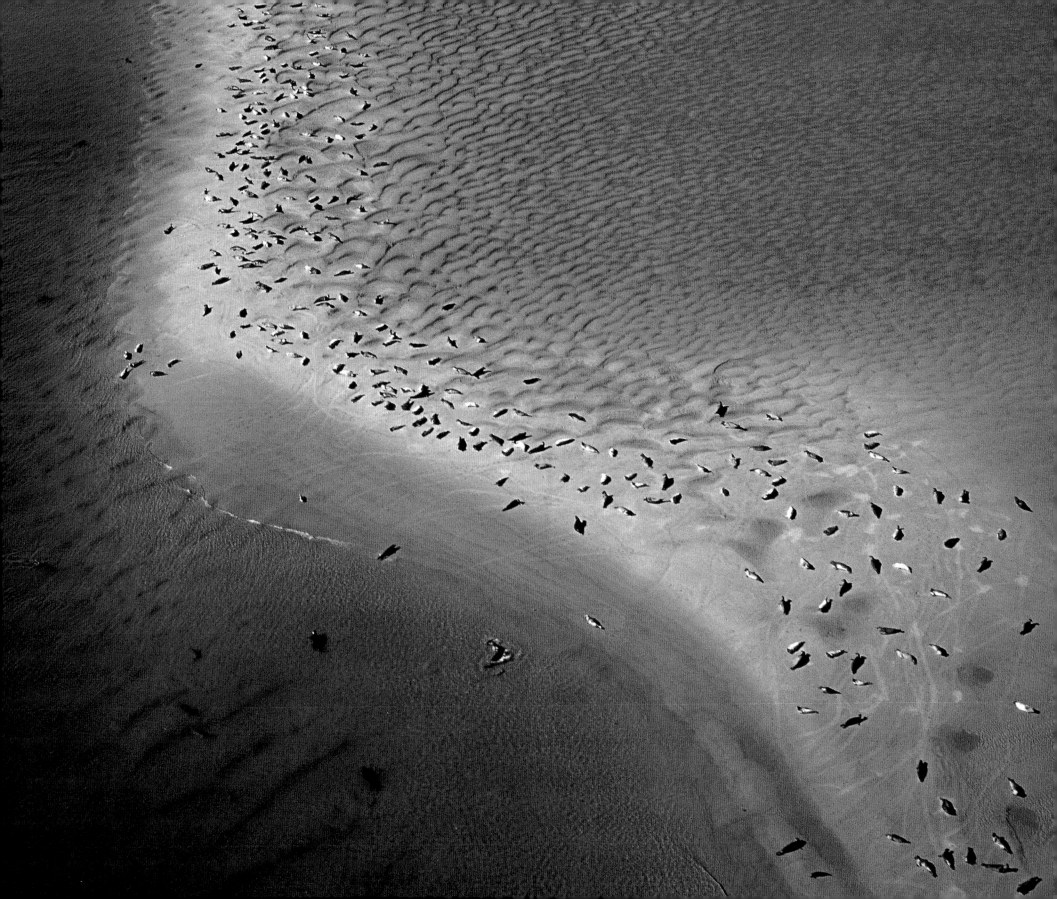

CLEY NEXT THE SEA

PEOPLE AND PLACE

Scenically Cley has everything a North Norfolk village should have! A famous windmill (star of the well known BBC trailer featuring the mill with drifting hot air balloon), a magnificent church of cathedral-like scale, traditional flint-walled and pantiled cottages and a wild backdrop of marshes and reedbeds. Shame today it lacks a village school, a bakery and a doctor's surgery though at least the village post office is still open. Cley in many ways is an icon of all that's traditionally North Norfolk and the subject of countless photos and artists' paintings.

Cley has many moods. In the short summer holiday season the narrow main street is full of hustle and bustle. The coast road narrows through the village and the sharp corner in the centre is really only suitable for a single line of traffic. This leads to frequent tail-backs and queues on busy weekends and Bank Holidays – perhaps not surprising when one considers this road was originally a route just for horses and carts delivering and collecting goods to and from Cley's once-busy harbour.

Outside holiday periods Cley is very different, quiet – perhaps too quiet – because of the high proportion of second and holiday homes which risk taking the heart out of the local community. However, throughout the year, the influx of birders on pilgrimage to the birdwatchers' mecca of Cley Marshes, as well as walkers drawn here by the light, colour and wildness of the coastal landscape, bring welcome all-season trade. Their revenues help sustain many B&Bs, an excellent pottery, several cafes and galleries and ensure that businesses such as the George Hotel, Picnic Fayre – an excellent delicatessen – and Cley's famous Smoke House seafood shop continue to thrive.

Undoubtedly the best way to explore Cley is on foot. Off the High Street discover the narrow lokes – passages between ancient flint walls – which run up to higher ground. Part of this area was the red light district when Cley was a busy port! On foot it's easy to spot many clues to Cley's history. The front of Whalebone House (now a vegetarian café) has bones not of whales but of sheep and horses in patterns among the flints – a reminder of the bonemeal fertilizer industry that flourished during the nineteenth century. No exploration of Cley would be complete without a walk to the famous windmill which milled flour from the early 1800s until the 1920s. It's now holiday accommodation but the interior can sometimes be visited on afternoons during the summer season. Equally Cley's church, St Margaret's of Antioch, with its magnificent windows, stonework, brasses and wonderful views across the River Glaven valley to Wiveton and Blakeney churches is essential visiting. The Three Swallows pub adjacent is an excellent refreshment stop.

Opposite: **Cley village – set between marshland and farmland.**

TIME AND TIDE

Cley may be a quiet village today but in medieval times it was a thriving fishing town, a busy international trading centre and, at its height, one of the greatest ports in England.

The narrow meandering River Glaven of today is a far cry from the original tidal estuary which at high tide flooded the valley between Cley and Wiveton. The river was once tidal as far inland as Glandford. Medieval Cley took ships up to 130 tons and Wiveton was a busy shipbuilding centre. Cley was the most important of the Haven ports – Cley, Blakeney, Wiveton and Salthouse. The original town and harbour were close to the medieval church, St Margaret's. After the great fire of Cley in September 1611, when 117 houses were destroyed, the town and wharves moved north towards the present High Street area, in part because silting of the Glaven restricted navigation higher up the river.

Cley remained for centuries an international trading centre and consequently also a notable smugglers' haunt. Its ships traded as far afield as Norway, Greece, Spain, France and Germany. Local Norfolk produce of barley, wheat, oats, wool, malt and oysters were important exports with ships returning with exotic cargoes of spices, fine cloths and wines. The trade with Rotterdam and the Low Countries was especially important. Today the Dutch influence is still visible in the curving Dutch gables on many Cley houses.

Cley was also an important fishing port. Cley fishermen ventured to waters as far away as Iceland. There were local oyster beds to be worked for the trade with London, and lobsters and crabs to be harvested from inshore waters. Associated with this trade was the demand for salt for packing and preserving fish. While much salt was imported there is also evidence of local salt production on Cley Marshes. Daniel Defoe writing in 1794 records 'large salt works in Cley which produce very good salt', and early OS maps show salt pans on the marshes edging the village.

The demise of this once great port was brought about by the silting of the Glaven estuary – not an entirely natural process but in large part due to land reclamation in the seventeenth and eighteenth centuries. As late as the 1800s trade continued but smaller boats, lighters, were used

to take goods for loading onto seagoing vessels anchored in the deeper water of Blakeney Pit. A typical lighter run with a four-man crew was a 14-hour round trip with a load of 45 tons of grain on the way out and 45 tons of coal back into Cley. The final nail in the coffin for this trade was the growth of King's Lynn as a major port and the development of the rail network, providing faster and cheaper inland transport.

Above: **Stained glass – St Margaret's church, Cley.**

FLOTSAM AND JETSAM

~ What's in a name? The name Cley simply means clay. Indeed there is always argument over whether the name of the village should be pronounced 'Cly' or 'Clay'. Both can be heard. 'Next to the Sea'? Well in medieval times, when the Glaven was a tidal estuary, Cley village really was next to the sea.

~ Cley Eye. The higher land alongside Beach road, now part of the Norfolk Wildlife Trust reserve, takes its name from the Old English term 'Eye' meaning an island. This higher ground was originally an island among tidal saltmarshes.

~ Plagued. The Black Death came to Cley in 1349. It is said that Norfolk's population fell by between a third and a half during plague years. The building of parts of St Margaret's church was delayed by its destructive effects, with the original plans never fully completed.

~ Buried in wool. Wool was the source of wealth that allowed the building of magnificent churches such as those at Cley, Salthouse and Blakeney. However, by the seventeenth century the industry was in decline. The Burial in Wool Acts of 1667 and 1679 were an unusual way of supporting a declining industry. The Acts made it law that, 'No corpse of any person, except those who shall die of the plague, shall be buried in any shirt, shift, sheet or shroud … or any stuff or thing other than what is made from sheep's wool only'. Churches, including St Margaret's at Cley, could fine any burial that contravened these Acts.

~ Many old houses in Cley are said to contain smugglers' holes where contraband was hidden from the King's Customs men.

~ Smugglers' haul. The Norfolk Chronicle of 16 December 1824 reports on the seizure of 120 half ankers of geneva (gin), 19 bags of tobacco and 10 bags of snuff in a confrontation with smugglers at Cley.

~ Iron constitution. The delicatessen 'Picnic Fayre' is on the site of the original village forge said to have been built in 1607 to make cannons for the English fleet. Look for the old anvil and beam drill in the shop!

~ The tall white-fronted building near Cley windmill was originally a Customs house built in 1680.

~ William White's Norfolk Directory of 1845 records passenger vessels sailing to London and Hull once a fortnight from Cley's harbour.

~ In 1570 Cley had 13 ships belonging to the town and 65 mariners.

~ Cley pirates. Sailors from Cley captured a Scottish ship bound for France in March 1406. On board was Prince James of Scotland. The eleven-year-old boy was sent to London where Henry IV held him hostage.

~ Cley pilgrims. The Glaven ports were licenced to carry pilgrims because of their closeness to Walsingham. In 1434 a ship from Cley took 60 pilgrims to the Shrine of St James the Apostle at Santiago de Compostella in Spain.

WILDERNESS AND WILDLIFE

Behind a storm-flung wall of shingle
A waving world of a million reeds and dappled waters

Cley Marshes hold a very special place in the history of British wildlife conservation. It was at the George Hotel, Cley, on Tuesday 14 March 1926, that Dr Sydney Long, who had purchased Cley Marshes for £5160 at auction a week earlier, held a meeting to form the Norfolk Naturalists' Trust, and to establish Cley Marshes as its first reserve. Thus began the County Wildlife Trust movement which today manages more than 2000 reserves nationally. The Trust founded by Sydney Long, now the Norfolk Wildlife Trust, is the largest of all the County Wildlife Trusts and manages more than 40 Norfolk reserves.

Cley reserve is famous for rare birds and it was here, in 1977, that avocets returned to Norfolk after an absence as regular breeders of more than 100 years. These marshes were well known to wildfowlers and

naturalists long before they were designated a reserve. In 1896 Edward Ramm shot a Pallas's Warbler at Cley – the first ever seen in Britain. Thus began a series of Cley 'firsts' which includes semi-palmated sandpiper, pacific swift, fan-tailed warbler, rock sparrow, and yellow-breasted bunting – all new to the British list and all adding to Cley's reputation as one of the UK's top birding sites.

When you visit the reserve today it is difficult to imagine that in medieval times this area was all tidal saltmarsh. In 1649 the land was reclaimed from the sea, the enclosures creating grazing land and freshwater marshes.

There are two very different worlds to experience on a walk around the reserve. The crunch of shingle underfoot and the sound of breakers characterises the beach area. Cley's shingle ridge is the best place to look for yellow horned-poppies and flocks of finches. The resident goldfinches and linnets are joined in winter by their attractive black and white

From far left:
One of Britain's rarest breeding birds –
a bittern in the reeds at Cley Marshes.
An otter swimming below the water's
surface in a dyke at Cley.
Ratty from *Wind in the Willows* – the
nationally rare water vole is still fairly
abundant at Cley.
Bearded tits are just one of the special
attractions of Cley Marshes to birdwatchers.

northern cousins, the snow buntings. Inland discover a quieter world
of waving reeds, cattle-grazed fields and shallow bird-haunted lagoons.
Cley's reedbeds are home to bitterns, bearded tits and marsh harriers
and in spring and autumn it's quite possible to see 20 species of wading
birds, including perhaps a wind-drifted rarity. In winter the marshes are
thronged with geese. Brent from Russia join the resident greylag and
Canada geese. Large numbers of migrant ducks, pintail and wigeon from
the north and east, also arrive in winter. Cley's famed East Bank is
perhaps the best location in Britain to learn wader and wildfowl
identification.

The marshes have been carefully managed for Norfolk Wildlife Trust
by three generations of the Bishop family. Robert, Billy and today Bernard
have wardened this site since the 1920s with the key to success being the
ability to control water levels through a series of linked sluices. Norfolk
reed is still cut in the traditional way on the reserve and sold for thatching.

*The 43 hectares of reeds at Cley form the largest reedbed on the North
Norfolk coast. Bitterns regularly breed here and this is one of the best sites
for watching bearded tits and marsh harriers. Norfolk Wildlife Trust's
thatched hides must rank as the most attractive and best designed of any
on the Norfolk coast. In spring and autumn they provide excellent views
of black-tailed godwits, spotted redshanks, curlew sandpipers and little
stints as well as commoner waders. Avocets breed in good numbers on the
lagoons. The shingle beach is a regular haunt of snow buntings and the sea
in winter often has divers, grebes, and auks close inshore. The freshwater
grazing marshes on both sides of the reedbeds are excellent for geese and
wildfowl with large numbers of brent geese and wigeon throughout the
winter. Otters and water voles frequent the dykes that edge the fields and
lapwing and golden plover flocks are also regular in the fields here.*

*The reserve is owned by Norfolk Wildlife Trust and the coastline here is
protected within the North Norfolk coast Site of Special Scientific Interest.*

REED HARVESTING AT CLEY

Norfolk reed has been harvested at Cley Marshes for generations and archaeologists have demonstrated that reed was used in England at least as long ago as 500 BC for thatching houses.

Around 7000 bundles of reed are cut at Norfolk Wildlife Trust's Cley reserve between mid-December and the end of February. The cutting is now done mechanically rather than with traditional reed-scythes but the cut reed is still cleaned by hand using a short wooden rake with six-inch nails forming the rake-head. The cleaned reed is then tied in bundles roughly three hand-spans in circumference.

Reed from Cley is not only sold to local thatchers but is valued right across England wherever there are cottages to thatch. Bundles have even been sold for use as far afield as Ireland.

At Cley, the drier areas of the reedbed are cut every year, which helps maintain the reedbed in good condition. When necessary, harvested areas are burnt to remove the reed-litter left after cutting. This helps ensure a pure stand of good quality reed for the following year.

Oppposite: **Cley's best-known landmark.**
Above: **Burning the reedbeds in winter prevents the build up of dead material.**
Below left: **Working the reedbeds at Cley – reedcutting.**
Below middle and right: **The bundled reeds will be sold for thatching.**

133

SALTHOUSE

PEOPLE AND PLACE

Salthouse, an evocative village name redolent of salt-laden northerly winds off the marshes, and a village which many times over the centuries has seen a 'rage' sweep the sea over the distant shingle beach ridge to flood marshes and homes alike.

The dominant feature of the village is the magnificent church of Saint Nicholas which stands guard over the flint-walled cottages that tumble down steep slopes towards the marshes below. Above the village lies Salthouse Heath, the best remaining heathland in North Norfolk and in the past a valued provider of grazing and heathland produce for the village, including fuel and rabbits!

Alongside the village green, and just off the busy main coast road is the excellent and historic pub, the Dun Cow, whose walls could tell many a smuggler's tale. Close by is Cookie's Crab Shop which specialises

in local seafood delicacies including marsh samphire gathered from local saltings – well worth a visit and it has a good tearoom too.

The village looks out over cattle-grazed freshwater marshes frequented by long-legged herons and tripod-bearing birdwatchers – the former in search of Salthouse's famous marsh eels and the latter for the bird rarities which arrive each spring and autumn.

Today, while few of the houses are still owned by families born in Salthouse, the village still retains the character and atmosphere unique to the North Norfolk coast. Its flint-walled cottages with red pantiled roofs, the vista of wild marshes thronged in winter with wildfowl and its cathedral-sized flint church could really be nowhere else. The views along the coast from Salthouse church, or even better from the heath above, are some of the best in North Norfolk.

Opposite: **St Nicholas's church stands guard over Salthouse village and looks out over marshes to the North Sea.**

Right: **A bulldozer pushes shingle onto the beach ridge at Salthouse.**

TIME AND TIDE

Archaeologists can extend the history of Salthouse at least back to Bronze Age times. Salthouse Heath has the largest assemblage of Bronze Age round barrows in North Norfolk. Some with evocative names such as 'Three Farthing' and 'Three Halfpenny' hills are clearly marked on the OS map for the area. Some of these barrows were excavated in the 1850s and urns of brown clay containing burnt bones typical of Bronze Age burials were removed. It is likely that even earlier, in Neolithic or even Mesolithic periods, prehistoric peoples were using the better-drained and more open land of the Cromer ridge as a hunting area. A number of Neolithic flints and hand axes have been found on Salthouse Heath. Nearby Kelling Heath is a rich site for the tiny flint points known as microliths. These indicate the production and repair of spears and arrows used for hunting in the period following the last Ice Age, some 10,000 years ago.

In medieval times the view from the village would have been rather different from today. The sea and shingle ridge would have been much further away and the land between the sea and the village would have been tidal saltmarsh dissected with muddy but navigable creeks. The view would have been much more akin to that from Blakeney village today.

Medieval Salthouse thrived as a fishing community with its boats having access to the sea along winding creeks through to Cley and Blakeney Pit. As well as fishing, Salthouse mariners were engaged in trading. Wool and corn were exported to the Low Countries. The lucrative nature of this trade is reflected in the size and richness of Salthouse church which was rebuilt in 1503 at a time when the wool trade prospered. We know from a Muster Roll of 1570 that at this time Salthouse had 38 mariners living in the village though it is unclear whether their ships anchored at Salthouse, or at Cley and Blakeney, which had better access to the sea.

Fishing and trade brought wealth to the village but for the poorer inhabitants the heath was as valuable as the sea. It provided rabbits for the pot, turves or flags to be burnt and common grazing for sheep, ponies and geese. These natural resources together with eels from the marshes and ducks, both domestic raised on the village pond (Salthouse was well known for its Aylesburys) and wild from the marshes, meant that in most years few villagers went hungry.

The Heath Award of 1781 gave rights for the poor of Salthouse to use the heath 'from this day forward for all time'. The enclosures at this time meant that much open land in the parish became the property of the Lord of the Manor. Salthouse Heath only survives today because of these rights granted to the poor of the parish. Parishioners whose houses had a rateable value of less than £10 had the right to pasture one cow, one heifer, one mare or foal or three calves and to cut flags, gorse and whin for their fires. In 1905 the rateable value to qualify was increased to £20 a year, though with modern house values it must be impossible for anyone to meet this requirement today.

No account of time and tide for Salthouse could be complete without mention of the periodic storm surges which several times a century have brought destruction of property and sometimes loss of life to the village. These are nothing new but the reclamation of the salt marshes which would have acted as a natural sea defence has worsened the problem. In the twentieth century the shingle beach barrier was overtopped by storms in 1938, 1953 and 1996. By far the most serious were the 1953 floods in which many Salthouse houses were damaged or destroyed and one woman lost her life. Pictures and accounts from the time show the scale of the disaster with Salthouse looking more like it had suffered a wartime bombing raid than a flood, so many houses having collapsed or lost walls.

Above: **A medieval sailing ship scratched on the back of a pew in St Nicholas's church – seventeenth century graffiti.**

FLOTSAM AND JETSAM

~ What's in a name? Salthouse or Salthus as recorded in the Domesday Book literally means a salt house. Was this a house where salt produced on the marshes was stored? This seems the most likely explanation though some argue that it was imported salt that was stored here to provision the local fishing industry and preserve their catches.

~ Salthouse church graffiti. Visit Salthouse church and you will find remarkable carvings on the choir stalls. These ancient graffiti probably date from the seventeenth century and illustrate three-masted sailing ships as well as carved initials and dates. Were they made by bored choirboys? Amazingly they have survived the centuries without an overzealous rector erasing them.

~ Salthouse held to ransom. In the late ninth century the towns of Sheringham and Salthouse had between them to find the annual sum of elevenpence as their contribution to the Danish King. This Danegeld for a number of years bought off the Viking raiders from across the North Sea.

~ Salthouse wreckers. In 1837 Salthouse villagers flocked to the tideline. The Raby Castle had been driven by a storm onto Salthouse beach and while the crew and passengers were saved, its cargo of spirits, wine, oranges, tea, and hampers was driven onto the shingle. Of the cargo valued at £5000 the coastguards recovered only £800 of goods, but in Salthouse the drinking was said to have continued for weeks!

~ The loss of a million tons of water. The reclamation of the marshes fronting Salthouse has in part brought about the silting of Cley and Blakeney channels. Spring tides would have covered the marshes with more than a million tons of water which as the tide ebbed would originally have flowed out through Cley and Blakeney channels scouring and deepening them and preventing deposits of silt and mud.

~ Salthouse Broads. During the First World War the Salthouse Marshes were deliberately flooded to prevent a German landing. The lakes produced became known by locals as the Salthouse Broads.

~ Mined where you walk. During the Second World War 18,000 mines were laid along the shingle bank by troops stationed in Salthouse: a dangerous job in which two servicemen died. Some locals say it was the bulldozing of the beach ridge at the end of the war to destroy mines that has permanently damaged its ability to act as a sea defence.

~ Punt guns on the marshes. In the early nineteenth century puntgunners regularly worked Salthouse marshes shooting huge numbers of wildfowl and waders. It is said that at the end of their wildfowling trips rather than make the effort of drawing charges from the gun muzzle they would fire on the avocets which still frequented the marshes at this time.

~ Salthouse international. During the Second World War Salthouse Heath had a dummy aerodrome complete with a revolving 'Lion' light to fool German aircraft into dropping their bombs here. There were also dummy tanks and lorries made from canvas.

~ Invading beaches. The shingle bank which protects Salthouse from the sea has been on the move for centuries. It has been moving inland at an average rate of a metre a year for at least the last 300 years. The shingle bank is pushed inland during tidal surges and storms.

~ Crusader hearts. At the one end of Salthouse church you will find a large unmarked slab of slate on the floor. It is reputed that two hearts are buried under this slab. It was not possible to bring the bodies of Crusaders back from the hot foreign climes in which they fought and so instead their hearts were brought back for burial.

WILDERNESS AND WILDLIFE

A lone heron waits and watches
as the white owl hovers over silver-headed reeds

Like Cley, Salthouse has had its share of bird rarities and its marshes were well known to Victorian collectors. This long tradition of rare vagrant visitors was continued in 1985 with the appearance of a little whimbrel, only the second ever to be recorded in Britain. Another less well-known claim to avian fame is that Salthouse marshes in 1941 became the first site in Britain for avocets to lay eggs after their extinction as a British breeding bird in the early nineteenth century.

Between the main coast road and the straight line of the coastal shingle bank lie extensive cattle-grazed freshwater marshes criss-crossed with reed-fringed dykes. Little egrets are now as much part of the bird scene here as the more familiar herons. In winter several thousand brent geese regularly congregate in the fields along with large numbers of wigeon, mallards and teals. In spring and summer sedge and reed warblers call loudly from the dykes and lapwings and redshanks perform their noisy and spectacular song flights over the marshland while skylarks sing high overhead. In April and May attractive yellow wagtails run busily around the feet of cattle, seeking insects. Sadly few of these passage birds remain to breed.

Behind the village of Salthouse the land slopes steeply upwards and less than a mile from the coastal marshes lies one of North Norfolk's finest heathlands. Even in mid-winter Salthouse Heath is bright with yellow gorse but visit in July and August and this is one of the most colourful landscapes in North Norfolk. The ground is richly patterned in purples, greens and yellows, carpeted with low-growing western gorse and bell heathers in full flower together. Elegant silver-barked birches stud the heathland and tracks and roads are fringed with a dense scrub of blackthorn, hawthorn, and young oaks.

Heathlands have a rich and specialised wildlife. Adders, common lizards and slow worms can still be found on Salthouse Heath. Birds include nightjars, stonechats, woodlarks and nightingales. May and June

are the best months to seek the heath's special birds. Visit at sunset on a warm, still evening when, as the light fades, the heath takes on a special magic. As other more common birds cease singing the nightingales come into their own, singing invisible, hidden among dense blackthorn scrub. As twilight fades the yellows and purples to a night time monochrome, the weird churrings of nightjars begin. Up to 2000 notes a minute are said to be produced in this strangest of bird songs. Look for woodcocks roding overhead on rounded wings. As it darkens the strange green fairy lights of glow-worms hidden in the undergrowth appear – all part of the special nature of this heathland world.

Salthouse Heath together with its neighbour Kelling Heath form the largest area of heathland in North Norfolk. The area of heathland was once much greater but over centuries, parts have been enclosed and 'improved' as farmland. The fragmented and isolated blocks of heathland that remain are only a fraction of their former extent and consequently much of their wildlife interest has been lost. It's difficult to believe that in former centuries Montagu's harriers regularly nested on Salthouse Heath and in winter white-tailed sea eagles hunted here. In the early 1900s Salthouse and Kelling heaths used to support a dozen pairs of red-backed shrikes, a species now extinct as a regular breeding bird in Britain.

Salthouse Heath is an ancient landscape. The presence of bronze age barrows and finds of stone-age flint tools are indicative of this. The Cromer Ridge – North Norfolk's upland – is formed from the sands and coarse flint gravels washed out from the edge of a vast continental ice

sheet that reached its southern limit here. The infertile and freely-drained soils, together with a history of grazing, burning and tree clearance that stretches back to the dawn of human history, have played a part in forming this heath.

139

Opposite: **A yellow wagtail has caught a dragonfly to feed its young – fields inland of Salthouse.**

Kissing's in season when gorse is in flower (Trad.)

Above left: **Winter on Salthouse Heath.**

Above: **Gorse flowering in summer on Salthouse Heath – Second World War defences in the background.**

WEYBOURNE

PEOPLE AND PLACE

Opposite: **Weybourne – yellow caterpillar-tracked tractors are used to launch and land crab boats on the steeply shelving pebble beach.**
Above: **Military re-enactment at the Muckleburgh Collection – Weybourne Camp.**

From the air it becomes obvious how the landscape of the North Norfolk coastline changes at Weybourne. The glacial cliffs which extend around the north-east coast of Norfolk begin here, running for 32 kms past Sheringham and Cromer to beyond Happisburgh. Formed from loose sands and gravels, the cliffs erode rapidly and the history of Weybourne, like that of Cromer and Sheringham, includes the loss of property on its seaward edge. There used to be a row of old coastguard cottages on the beach and for many years one was run as a beach café known as 'Angela's Ark'. However, these were lost to erosion by the 1940s.

Today Weybourne's shingle beach is popular with birdwatchers, walkers and fishermen. Many fishing competitions are organised here and the fishermen's tents and windbreaks are a distinctive sight along the beach. Even more distinctive are the ancient, yellow, caterpillar-tracked

tractors which pull the crab boats up and down the beach. There are still four or five boats here with their two-man crews making a living out of crab and lobsters.

While the village only has a single shop it can boast several attractions which draw visitors. The Muckleburgh Collection, just along the coast road from the village, is home to the largest private collection of military vehicles in the UK as well as having an amazing collection of military paraphernalia on show including rocket launchers, field guns, and ack-ack guns. Just inland from the village is a carefully restored railway station, now used by the North Norfolk Railway, which runs steam and diesel trains between Sheringham and Holt. What makes Weybourne special is its setting: flint cottages and a windmill backed by the wooded hills and valleys of the Cromer ridge and fronted by the harsh North Sea.

TIME AND TIDE

He who would old England win,
Must at Weybourne Hoop begin
(Trad.)

Weybourne has a long and rather surprising history of military fortifications stretching back to at least the time of the Spanish Armada and perhaps even beyond to the days of Danish and Viking incursions along this stretch of the Norfolk coast. The reason for this lies in the steeply sloping beach and deep water close inshore which has always raised fears that invaders could land troops here.

A map dated 1588 shows a fort here and in the same year the Holt parish register records,

'in this year was the town of Waborne fortified with a continuall garrison of men bothe of horse and foote with sconces (earthworks), ordinaunce and all manner of appointment to defend the Spannyards landing theare'.

Similarly when England feared invasion by the French in Napoleonic times artillerymen were stationed on the cliffs here. During both the First and Second World Wars Weybourne was heavily defended. Concrete pillboxes from the Second World War are prominent along the shoreline though many have already been lost to erosion and others near the cliff edge will undoubtedly follow in the next few years.

In 1935 Weybourne Camp was developed as an anti-aircraft gunnery training centre. Catapult-launched pilotless aircraft known as 'Queen Bees' were used for target practice. During war years many troops were stationed at Weybourne. By the time the Camp finally closed in 1958 it is estimated that 1,500,000 shells had been fired out to sea and several hundred thousand troops had been trained here.

The village today is rather more sedate than at many periods in its past: piracy, smuggling, military bases and Viking raiders all feature in the coast's history here. In the nineteenth and early twentieth centuries the village would have supported far more trades than today. Certainly in the mid 1800s there were fishermen, farmworkers, a thatcher, miller, grocer, cattle-dealer, coal-carter, coastguards, net-braider, shepherds, blacksmiths, a rat-catcher, gamekeeper, dressmaker and needlewoman living here and businesses included a brewery, fish curing, and a malting house. What a contrast with today!

Above: **Weybourne's village sign features a windmill, a horse and cart and a steam train on the North Norfolk railway.**

142

FLOTSAM AND JETSAM

~ What's in a name? At the time of the Domesday Book the settlement was named Wabrunna. It is suggested that this name means 'the stream of the felons' indicating a place where thieves and criminals were drowned. This practice continued in England up until the fifteenth century.

~ We will fight them on the beaches. Winston Churchill visited Weybourne in June 1941 to observe the testing of a prototype anti-aircraft missile. The event was not a complete success as the unmanned target plane was eventually destroyed only after the camp's artillery guns opened fire.

~ Weybourne under attack. Despite its long history of military fortifications the only time in recorded history that Weybourne has come under direct attack was on the 11 July 1940. A Luftwaffe plane bombed the camp and the village and while no-one was killed several houses were damaged.

~ Of shells and shellfish. The proposal to establish an artillery training camp here in the mid 1930s was fiercely opposed by local fishermen as the sea off Weybourne was considered to be one of the best crab and lobster fishing grounds on the east coast of England.

~ Brandy and baccy. Weybourne was a notorious area for smuggling from medieval times through to the nineteenth century. This was because the deep water offshore allowed large vessels to lay close to the shore from where contraband could easily be offloaded to small rowing boats. Local farmers could supplement their incomes by hiring their horses and carts to smugglers' gangs which sometimes numbered over 100 people using 20 to 30 horse-drawn carts. There was so much smuggling at Weybourne that a preventative boat and coastguards were stationed here. However, legend has it that Weybourne smugglers would bury themselves under the shingle with only their mouths and noses showing, making themselves invisible until after the custom's men had passed. A wide range of goods was smuggled, though chief amongst these were geneva (gin) and tobacco. A list of goods seized at Weybourne in the 1700s also includes rum, brandy, tea, silks, firearms and gunlocks.

~ Weybourne's power station. In the 1960s Weybourne was proposed as a possible location for a nuclear power station because of the availability of deep sea water close inshore for cooling. Fortunately it was soon realised that building a nuclear power station on a site with rapidly eroding cliffs would not be very sensible!

143

Above left: **A male grey partridge calls in a stubble field at Weybourne.**

Above right: **Young grey partridges huddle together – farmland at Weybourne.**

Opposite left: **Looking east along the cliffs at Weybourne.**

Opposite right: **Sand martins nesting in cliff holes at Weybourne.**

WILDERNESS AND WILDLIFE

Waves sigh, pebbles clatter.
White foam below brown cliffs

At Weybourne the character of the Norfolk coast changes. The shingle, saltmarshes and sand dunes which weave their ever-changing patterns all the way between Holme and Blakeney are replaced here by stark, flint-encrusted, brown cliffs. The beach shelves steeply and is composed of shingle and large rounded flints worn smooth by the sea. This beach is a hostile environment for plant and animal life as tides and waves constantly move the shingle, preventing any plant life from establishing itself. Birds on the beach are more likely to be resting than feeding. There are usually herring and great black-backed gulls either on the beach or bobbing in the water just offshore. Small parties of waders – turnstones, ringed plovers and oystercatchers – often fly along the shore seeking better feeding grounds or find a high tide roost among the flints.

The cliffs between here and Sheringham are almost vertical, but where there are suitable ledges, fulmars nest. They were first noted here in the 1940s and pupils from Gresham's school in Holt cut artificial ledges to encourage them to stay. The first successful nesting of fulmars in Norfolk took place here in 1947, and today more than 100 pairs can be found on the cliffs between here and Sheringham. Another species which takes advantage of the soft, crumbling cliffs is the sand martin. They breed in colonies, each pair excavating a nest tunnel in suitable sandy parts of the cliff. In places, just below the cliff tops, vertical sand faces are pock-marked with their holes.

The Norfolk coast path follows the cliff tops from Weybourne to Sheringham. Most of the cliff top fields are arable land, but edging the cliffs is a fringe of grassland. In spring and summer common blue butterflies and red and black burnet moths dance over clumps of pink sea thrift. Kestrels hang on the updrafts above the cliffs then dive on half-folded wings to well-hidden cliff nest sites. When the sun shines there always seem to be skylarks in song and in wintertime the farmland here attracts flocks of larks, pipits and the occasional party of snow buntings.

The only road to the beach at Weybourne ends at a car park used by fishermen. This is close to a small reedbed and pool immediately behind the shore. In summer there are reed warblers, sedge warblers and several pairs of coots nesting here. In the past bitterns have been seen, and at migration times it's well worth checking the surrounding area for migrants. Wheatears and whinchats are regular in spring and autumn.

Weybourne cliffs are a Site of Special Scientific Interest (SSSI), but mainly for their geological rather than their wildlife interest. In autumn gales the cliffs provide a vantage point to observe seabirds. Gannets, skuas and kittiwakes can be expected in northerly winds. The cliff tops in spring and autumn have produced some notable bird rarities, including alpine accentor, short-toed lark, pied wheatear, wryneck, hoopoe, Richard's pipit and tawny pipit. The scrub-covered slopes of Muckleburgh Hill are a well-known site for nightingales and a mile inland Kelling Heath, like Salthouse Heath, is rich in heathland birds, animals and plants. (See Salthouse section for details.)

Above: **Skylark feeding young amongst scarlet pimpernels – fields at Weybourne.**
Opposite: **A hare bounds over cliff-top fields near Weybourne.**

SHERINGHAM

PEOPLE AND PLACE

Opposite: **Evening light – the fishermen's slipway and the promenade.**
Above and right: **The potty festival takes over the High Street in Sheringham.**

There are two Sheringhams: the pretty village of Upper Sheringham lying in a fine position on the north facing slope of the Cromer ridge below the woodlands of Sheringham Park, and the vastly larger town of Sheringham built on the soft coastal cliffs and protected from winter storms by its concrete sea walls and promenades. Upper Sheringham today has just a few hundred inhabitants in contrast to the more than 7000 residents of Sheringham town. It is hard to credit that for most of its long history Upper Sheringham was the primary settlement and Lower Sheringham little more than an outpost where fishermen could launch their boats and land their catches.

The decline of Sheringham's importance for fishing has been more than matched by its growth as a tourist centre. Today fewer than 20 boats work from Sheringham beach and the majority of these are on a part-time basis. The tiny numbers employed in fishing contrasts starkly with the many hundreds of local jobs dependent directly and indirectly on servicing tourism.

Sheringham boasts many attractions for visitors. Its beach, though topped by shingle and flints, has excellent sands and as the tide falls there are safe clean pools to paddle in. Many come to enjoy the summer carnival and since 1994 in the first week of July it hosts the Potty Festival. This exhibition of crazy costumes and madcap dancing was started by local morris dancers. The North Norfolk Railway, managed by local enthusiasts, runs steam trains and locomotives along the 'Poppy Line' to Weybourne and Holt. Sheringham Park, close to Upper Sheringham, is another honeypot for visitors. Owned now by the National Trust, it was originally the family seat of the Upcher family. The park has fantastic views over the North Norfolk coast and in May and June the rhododendrons and azaleas in full flower are spectacular, creating a sea of colours and scents.

The Henry Ramey Upcher lifeboat, dating from 1894, and the rudder from Sheringham's first lifeboat the *Augusta* (built in 1838), can be viewed at the small lifeboat museum at the top of Fishermen's Slope. Nearby one of Sheringham's oldest pubs, the Two Lifeboats, is well worth a visit and its sign depicts the *Augusta*. The building has been at various times a coffee house, a brothel and a Baptist reading room.

Sheringham's town coat of arms shows a golden lobster and, despite the decline in the fishing industry, you can still watch small boats being hauled up onto Sheringham beach to unload their catches of lobsters and crabs. In recent years the catch returns, which include boats operating from Weybourne and the Runtons, show more than 50,000 kg of crabs and 4,000 kg of lobsters are landed each year.

TIME AND TIDE

The land and the sea, farming and fishing: these have for centuries been the mainstays of Sheringham livelihoods.

In the twelfth century the adjacent settlement of Beeston Regis was more important than Upper Sheringham. The Augustinian Priory there, established in 1197, provided a place of hospitality for travellers and pilgrims on route to Walsingham. The ruins of this priory are still visible.

Upper Sheringham was the original settlement and Lower Sheringham simply a place with a freshwater stream and a gap in the cliffs where residents of Upper Sheringham could launch their fishing boats and land their catches. The original wooden fishermen's huts were soon replaced by simple flint and pebble cottages and the complimentary trades of rope-making and fish-curing became established. However, even by the time of Faden's Map in 1797, Upper Sheringham remained the larger settlement and Lower Sheringham was just a small grouping of fishermen's and fish merchants' flint and pebble cottages. In 1836 White's Directory records 26 herring boats, many smaller boats and six fish-curing houses based here.

Because of the lack of a harbour at Sheringham catches were often transferred at sea to larger vessels. These took Sheringham crabs and lobsters direct to London markets.

By 1870 there were said to be 200 boats at Sheringham, mainly small inshore boats, but including a few larger deep sea fishing boats. This led to considerable congestion and the competition for safe places to haul out boats caused several fishing families to leave Sheringham entirely.

The first few Victorian tourists came to stay in Sheringham from the 1870s but it was only when the rail link was completed on 16 June 1887 that visitors began to flock to Sheringham. Development was extremely rapid and by the 1890s there were several large hotels and of course the cliff top golf links. Sheringham golf club opened in 1892 with the course extended to 18 holes in 1898. Though these developments soon led to Lower Sheringham becoming the larger settlement, the church of All Saints, at Upper Sheringham, remained the Parish church for both Sheringhams until 1953.

Above: **Upper Sheringham's village sign depicts a lifeboat - wooden boats like these were once built in Upper Sheringham**

FLOTSAM AND JETSAM

~ What's in a name? In the Domesday Book of 1086 the settlement of Upper Sheringham was recorded as 'Silingham'. By the twelfth century it was known as Siringham and by the late thirteenth century as Schyringham. The name is of Scandinavian origin and means the home of Scira's people.

~ The Sheringham mermaid. The tale goes that during a service at All Saint's church, Upper Sheringham, a mermaid tried to enter the church. She was thrown out but managed to creep back in and seated herself on the pew nearest the door. Today you can still see her as there is a carving of her decorating the pew that she sat on. She is also shown on the village sign outside the church.

~ Watering places. Both Upper and Lower Sheringham have very special water sources used by those who didn't have their own well. The clock tower, a distinctive building on Sheringham High Street, was built originally to supply water and had a horse trough on one side and a public tap on the other. Upper Sheringham still has its public reservoir outside the church. This was erected in 1814 and was the only public source of water until the late 1950s when the village was connected to mains water.

~ Whelk coppers. The tearoom on the seafront promenade is named Whelkcoppers because during the 1920s and 1930s whelks were boiled in large copper vessels here. Sheringham was a major supplier of whelks to London but the trade died out during the Second World War as fishermen were no longer allowed to work the sea bed off Weybourne because of military activity.

~ Zeppelin Raids. Sheringham has the distinction of being the first place in Britain to be bombed from the air. On 19 January 1915 a German Zeppelin air ship dropped two incendiary bombs on the town. Parts of one bomb can be seen in the town museum!

~ Sheringham stone breakers. For many years winter employment was provided for fishermen's families in the back-breaking job of collecting flints from the beach. These were supplied to the Stoke on Trent pottery industry. In the 1930s about 4500 tons of blue flints were removed from the beach each year and pickers were paid about six shillings a ton. As late as the 1960s there was still a trade in flints with 2500 tons a year being taken. This was finally stopped in 1969 because of fears that it was adding to beach erosion.

~ The cannon in Gun Street. At the bottom of the High Street on the corner with Gun Street, Sheringham's cannon can still be seen. This may date from the time of the Spanish Armada in 1588 or perhaps from 1673 when there were fears of a Dutch invasion.

~ Shannocks: the name for inhabitants of Sheringham. To be a proper Shannock you must be born in Sheringham and have parents also born and bred here.

~ Sheringham's great sewer explosion. In 1903 shortly after the introduction of a mains sewage system there was a huge explosion on the promenade resulting in three deaths and several injuries. A tank under the promenade linked to the sewage pipe running across the beach exploded because of a build-up of methane gas. It is said that the force of the explosion was so great that shock waves caused cliff falls as far away as Beeston Regis.

WILDERNESS AND WILDLIFE

Ebb and flow, wind and wave
A tide-line treasure trove of gleaming flints

The undulating countryside and coastline at Sheringham have a more intimate character than the flat, open marshland coast further west. Some of the steep wooded valley sides and shady, sunken lanes above Upper Sheringham and the Runtons feel more akin to Devon than the stereotype of 'flat' Norfolk. The belt of woodlands south of Sheringham extends from the Great Wood at Felbrigg Park, through Roman Camp and Beeston Regis to Sheringham Park and Weybourne Wood. This forms the most extensive area of woodland anywhere along the North Norfolk coast.

Several of these woodlands are owned by the National Trust and throughout the area there is a good network of public footpaths. These woodlands are varied, ranging from plantations of conifers to mixed woodlands, overgrown heaths of birch and pine, and some fine coastal oak woods carpeted in parts with bluebells. Grey squirrels, roe and muntjac deer, badgers, foxes, stoats and weasels can all be found in this area, though in general wild mammals are more elusive than woodland birds. Buzzards have recently increased in numbers and are no longer an uncommon sight soaring over the woods, sparrowhawks nest and even the rare goshawk has been recorded here. Sheringham Park is as good a spot as any for the commoner woodland birds including nuthatches, treecreepers, green and great spotted woodpeckers, jays, numerous pheasants, goldcrests and long-tailed tits. Woodcocks are not unusual in winter but only very small numbers remain in spring to breed.

The town of Sheringham has developed quite a reputation among birdwatchers as a site for autumn sea-watching. The shelters along the sea-front promenade provide convenient look-outs and in northerly gales storm-driven seabirds including shearwaters, gannets, guillemots, razorbills, skuas and divers pass offshore.

Another wildlife gem of Sheringham is Beeston Regis common. This lies on the eastern edge of the town and is easily accessed by footpaths off the A149 coast road. It is a magical overgrown area of wet heathland with wonderful displays of orchids in spring. There is a small pond with a convenient seat where you can watch large dragonflies hawking over the water and spot frogs, toads and even the occasional grass snake. For botanists this is one of the richest small sites in North Norfolk with over 100 species of flowering plants including many unusual species.

Previous page left: **In spring bluebells carpet many woodlands inland of Sheringham.**
Previous page right: **Rhododendrons create a magnificent display at Sheringham Park in June.**
Right: **Weasels are common in North Norfolk but difficult to observe.**

The National Trust protects and manages large areas of woodland in the Sheringham area. Sheringham Park was purchased by the National Trust in 1987 and its undulating oak woodlands have dramatic views down to the coastline. The park was laid out by the famous nineteenth century landscape designer Humphry Repton. He described Sheringham Park as his 'most favourite work'.

The National Trust also own and manage the wooded heaths of Beacon Hill, the Roman Camp and Beeston Regis Heath. In spring there are some beautiful carpets of bluebells within the beech, oak and birch woodland here. Management work by the National Trust has also restored small areas of heathland within these woodlands helping to ensure the survival of adders and the return of nightjars.

The 1700 acres of Felbrigg Estate, south-east of Sheringham, include both woodland and parkland. There are magnificent seventeenth century sweet chestnuts and ancient beech pollards. Felbrigg's Great Wood is protected as a Site of Special Scientific Interest (SSSI) and the beech woodland here is thought to be at the northern limit of this tree's natural range in Britain. The woodland and parkland trees are rich in lichens with almost 100 species recorded.

Right: **A great spotted woodpecker looks for insects on a dead birch tree –
Sheringham Park.**

EAST AND WEST RUNTON

PEOPLE AND PLACE

Runton is unusual as a village divided into East and West. Originally simply referred to as Runton, the two parts have in recent times developed separate identities and are now best considered as two villages still within a single parish.

The first impression of East Runton as you drive along the coast road from Cromer is of the large and rather unsightly caravan parks on the cliff tops. Indeed, it is easy to drive past both East and West Runton with barely a glance. Stop and explore the hinterland. You will discover two extremely attractive villages with commons, duck ponds, and some lovely old flint fishermen's cottages backed by some of the best countryside anywhere on the North Norfolk coast. Behind both Runtons lie some wonderful, narrow lanes with ferns encrusting their high banks as they cut through the steeply sloping hillside woods of the Cromer ridge. Once referred to as 'The Switzerland of East Anglia', a slightly exaggerated title to be sure, the parish can claim the highest land in Norfolk. Roman

Camp and Beacon Hill reach the dizzying heights of 330 ft. Parts of this area are owned by the National Trust and a good network of footpaths through the Roman Camp and Incleborough Hill heaths and woods offer fine views along the coast to Sheringham and Cromer.

The holiday trade supports a concentration of good restaurants and pubs in the Runtons including the well-known Greek restaurant Constantia in East Runton and the famous Mirabelle in West Runton. The most striking of the hotels is the Links Hotel next to West Runton's 100-year-old golf course.

Apart from the beach the main visitor attraction is the Shire Horse Centre in West Runton, home to the best collection of heavy horses in the country. On demonstration days you can get a feel for how farming was practiced here before the 1950s when horses ploughed and harrowed the fields and were an essential part of the rural economy.

Small fishing boats still work from Woman's Hythe at West Runton and East Runton gap and are towed up and down the beach on ancient and extremely battered tractors. East and West Runton settlements owe their origins to these two gaps in the cliffs which allowed fishing communities to develop here and still provide the only safe access onto the beach today.

It's well worth venturing off the main road to explore these villages. In East Runton you can still find the village common grazed by flocks of white geese and marvel at the two massive nineteenth century railway viaducts, one redundant but the other still in use by trains on the Sheringham to Norwich line.

Opposite: **Eroding cliffs between East and West Runton.**
Above left: **Suffolk Punches are just one of the heavy horse breeds which can be seen at West Runton's Shire Horse Centre.**
Above right: **Fishing boats are towed up and down the beach by tractors at East Runton.**

TIME AND TIDE

An elephant at West Runton! Well, it was 500,000 years ago when bears, hyenas, rhinos and sabre-toothed cats were also part of the local scene. West Runton has been famous since the nineteenth century for fossils found at the base of the cliffs in a layer known as the West Runton Freshwater Bed. This is part of the Cromer Forest Bed dating from over half a million years ago and named after the periodic finds of fossil tree stumps in this deposit.

The find which made West Runton internationally famous was made on 13 December 1990 by Harold and Margaret Hems who were walking along the beach after a storm and spotted a large bone projecting from the base of the cliff. This was identified as belonging to an extinct species of elephant. More bones, revealed after storms in winter 1991, suggested that a complete elephant skeleton might be present. Investigations were begun by Cromer and Norwich museums with some parts of the skeleton removed in 1992. Then a major dig in 1995 removed thousands of tonnes of overlying sand and gravels from the cliff. The result of these 'mammoth' efforts was the preservation of a near-complete skeleton of an elephant that would have stood four metres tall and weighed about ten tons – twice the weight of a modern African elephant.

The eroding cliffs at Runton, which are cut back by storms and retreat an average of one metre a year have produced more than just fossils. At the West Runton gap known as Woman's Hythe, finds have been made of Neolithic, Bronze Age, Iron Age, Romano-British and medieval pottery showing a history of human use of the area extending back millennia.

The Runton villages have over time retreated with the cliffs and there are records from the fourteenth century onwards of the loss of many houses to erosion. The tithe map of 1840 shows six cottages and a wash house on the cliff top which had all been lost by 1885. Indeed, even the buildings which replaced these had also disappeared shortly after the First World War. In former centuries it was not unusual for buildings simply to be dismantled and re-erected further inland.

From medieval times farming and fishing were the mainstays of Runton's community with the local economy based on sheep, corn and fishing and a little smuggling thrown in for good measure. The cliff-top fields, now occupied by caravans, were 'half year' lands tilled in the summer but open for communal grazing between Michaelmas and Lady Day. This centuries-old tradition was maintained until the late 1970s with the caravans being removed over winter. Sadly, a legal enquiry in 1975 and 1976 did not confirm these common rights and now the caravans have sprouted balconies and legs and become a permanent fixture – at least until the sea encroaches!

As at Cromer the transformation of the Runtons into holiday resorts started slowly with wealthy London families coming to spend the summer season here from the early 1800s. However the success of the gangs of 'navigators' who dug the cuttings between Holt and Cromer brought a station to West Runton in September 1887 and a rapid influx of visitors led to the opening of several large hotels such as West Runton's Links hotel in 1899 and the letting of many cottages to the holiday trade.

Today, with former industries of brick-making, and fish-smoking long gone, tourism is now the major occupation. Many former holiday-makers are choosing to retire here, attracted by the peace and beauty of the surrounding countryside.

Above: **West Runton's village sign illustrates both the past importance of fishing to the local community and the finding of its fossil elephant.**

FLOTSAM AND JETSAM

~ What's in a name? Runton simply means Run's settlement or was the original settler named Runa of Rune? In the Domesday book Runton was recorded as Runetuna.

~ What did the Romans ever do for Runton? Well as far as Roman Camp, the area of woodland and heath above West Runton goes, the answer may be not a lot. There is no evidence of Roman activity here but it was however a major iron working area in Saxon and medieval times.

~ Wreck of the Sea. In medieval times the rights to goods and materials washed ashore (known as wreck of the sea) were jealously guarded. At Runton these rights were split between the Lords and Priors of Beeston and Felbrigg. The records of 1392 show 40 barrels of beer (20 empty and 20 full), 46 planks of wood, one oak tree, part of a ship, one windlass, ship's spars and steering oars were salvaged from Runton beach.

~ Golfing coup. West Runton's golf course was established in 1903 but its claim to fame must surely be the golfing coup of appointing the world famous golfer, Gary Player, as its director in 1979.

~ The Switzerland of East Anglia. In the early 1900s Runton became known as the Switzerland of East Anglia and built its reputation as a health resort for its 'exceedingly salubrious and bracing' air.

~ When elephants walked at Runton. Fossil mammals found at West Runton include steppe mammoth (elephant), Barbary macaque, beaver, wolf, bear, spotted hyena, wild boar, sabre-toothed cat, red deer, elk, wild horse and rhinoceros. All date from the period around 500,000 to 700,000 years ago.

~ Smugglers tales. The commons and heaths above Runton were great hiding places for contraband. In February 1793 customs and excise men seized twelve-and-a-quarter hundredweight of tea hidden among gorse on Runton heath. The deep waters between Sheringham and Weybourne allowed smugglers' vessels to anchor close to shore and transfer contraband to the smaller boats that could land at Runton Gap. In December 1823 the Sheringham preventative boat seized 87 half ankers of geneva (gin) and casks of tobacco on West Runton beach.

~ Shire-horse giants. At the West Runton Shire Horse Centre visitors can see the horses which for generations tilled the land before the Fordson tractors of the 1930s began to supplant them. At 19 hands (over six feet high) and weighing more than a ton these are among the heaviest and strongest horses in the world.

~ West Runton rockers. Sleepy West Runton seems a highly unlikely setting for concerts by some of the most notorious rock bands. However during the early 1970s bands including the Sex Pistols played at West Runton Pavilion – at least until it burnt down!

Above: **East Runton's village sign shows crab boats being launched beneath the cliffs at Runton Gap.**

WILDERNESS AND WILDLIFE

Under dark flints in white rock pools
hermit crabs hide in borrowed hard shells

As the tide falls at West Runton a very special shore world of white chalk rock pools and strangely-shaped flints is gradually revealed. This is a miniature wildlife wilderness, occupying just a few acres of shore, but home to some of the most extraordinary creatures to be found anywhere along the North Norfolk coastline.

The low waters of spring tides, when the sea retreats furthest from the shore, are the best time to explore this slippery world. The weird and wonderful array of flints provide refuge in their nooks and crannies for some equally weird and wonderful marine creatures. Under the lips of rock overhangs are the pink, jelly-like blobs of sea anemones and strangely-coloured encrustations of sponges. Hiding under seaweeds or beneath flints in the small rock pools several species of crab can be found. Small hermit crabs scuttle across the pool bottoms protected by their whelk-shell armour. Shore crabs come in a range of colours – greens, browns and blacks. The large orange edible crabs, found in pools lower down the shore, sport spectacularly large pincers which can give a nasty nip. Velvet swimming crabs display wonderful purple-blue markings on their legs and dance aggressively with sideways steps and pincers held high when disturbed.

The best way to observe this rock pool world is simply that … to observe. A few minutes peering into the water reveals the translucent bodies of prawns and shrimps and the extraordinary camouflage of blennies and gobies. I have found strange spiny scorpion fish hidden in the deeper pools. Their dorsal spines contain a powerful venom and should not be handled.

The range of marine life varies with tide and season. Late summer is a good time to find squat lobsters whereas winter brings more starfish including the less common brittle stars. The seaweeds here include the slippery brown bladder and spiral wracks. Part their fronds to reveal periwinkles on the rocks and perhaps a sea slater, marine relative of the woodlouse, scuttling away out of the light.

Bird life along the shore here can be quite varied. The rocky shore with its wealth of life provides feeding grounds for turnstones, oyster-catchers and gulls. The waders can be remarkably difficult to spot among the jumbled flints. The crumbling brown cliffs which back the beach offer nesting sites to pairs of fulmars and colonies of sand martins and the cliff top fields often have wheatears present in spring and autumn.

The foreshore below the beach at West Runton is the only chalk rocky shore between Flamborough Head in Yorkshire and the north Kent coast. It is an oasis for rock pool life. West Runton cliffs are a Site of Special Scientific Interest (SSSI) primarily for their record of the last Ice Age and extraordinary fossils but also for the area's rocky shore wildlife interest.

160

Opposite: At the coast the light changes from moment to moment – silver sea and a weather front viewed from West Runton beach looking towards Cromer Pier.

Quiet lanes above the Runtons are rich in wildlife.

Opposite: A fox has found a pheasant's nest on a lane-side bank. Clockwise from top: After heavy rain this male yellowhammer takes advantage of a puddle to bathe in. Harvest mice are secretive but not uncommon along field margins. A tawny owl in woodland above West Runton. Muntjac deer have increased in numbers and are now found in many woodlands in North Norfolk.

CROMER

PEOPLE AND PLACE

Oh I do love to be beside the seaside,
I do love to be beside the sea
I do love to walk along the prom-
prom-prom ...
John A Glover-Kind

I'm the on'y one on Cromer pier this
February day, An what they call a lazy
wind is whippin' up the spray. That lazy
wind, that crazy wind, from icy seas
come tew yer. Tha's jus' tew lazy to go
round, an' so that go clean trew yer!
Lazy wind by John Kett

Cromer is best known for its crabs and its pier. These reflect the two major influences on its development: fishing and tourism. At heart it remains a traditional English seaside resort, one of the few still retaining an end-of-pier 'Seaside Special' summer show. This traditional variety show with its blend of comedy, singing and dancing attracts more than 40,000 visitors to the pier's Pavillion Theatre each summer season, though it's reputed that overall the pier has never made a penny profit since it was first built over 100 years ago. Cromer's pier is the genuine article, a pukka pier complete with Lifeboat Station at its seaward end. Since it opened in 1900 it's been a place to promenade and what better place even today to watch the waves roll by, peer in the buckets of children crabbing with baited lines, or simply sit in the shelter of its pavilioned seats and enjoy the sunset?

The pier isn't the only attraction. Visitors to Cromer can enjoy exploring the old centre of town – a maze of narrow streets around its parish church, St. Peter and Paul's. You certainly can't miss the church. Its 160 ft tower is visible from almost everywhere in Cromer and is the highest in Norfolk.

On fine summer days Cromer's safe sandy beaches are busy with families with young children and if the weather is bad there is always the cinema. Cromer is the only North Norfolk coastal town still retaining a cinema. Other attractions include two museums and the cliff top golf course. Not far away is Felbrigg Hall, owned by the National Trust, with magnificent parkland walks and ancient woodlands.

For the best view of Cromer climb the church tower, a slightly dizzying experience, or walk along the eastern cliffs to the lighthouse which stands on a vantage point with superb views both over the town and out to sea. Cromer is much more than just a summer holiday resort. It has grown over the last 100 years into the largest town on the North Norfolk coast. Its population of over 8000 exceeds that of Sheringham, Wells or Hunstanton and it is the administrative headquarters for North Norfolk with the District Council offices located here.

Opposite: **View looking west over Cromer towards East Runton.**
Above: **Crab boat running the waves at Cromer beach.**
Below: **In recent years both Cromer and East Runton have become popular with surfers.**

TIME AND TIDE

Cromer has a long history as a small fishing settlement and a much shorter one as a fashionable resort town. Its story begins with that of another town, Shipden. You won't find Shipden on any modern map as this fishing and trading settlement, situated seaward of Cromer, disappeared under the waves by the late fourteenth century. It is said that until the nineteenth century, on very low tides, the remains of the church of St Peter, Shipden could still be seen. Then in 1888, the paddle steamer *Victoria*, on its way out of Cromer, foundered on Church rock as the remains of the church had become known. No lives were lost but the *Victoria* was wrecked (not too many ships can have sunk after hitting a church!) and attempts were made to destroy the 'rock' with explosives.

Shipden was lost to cliff erosion, with its church succumbing around 1390. Its residents were granted land in an area known at the time as Crowsmere. The name stuck and modern Cromer takes its name from this.

The problem for Cromer, as for Shipden before it, is the lack of any natural harbour for its fishing boats. Boats had to be pulled up onto the beach to unload and for safekeeping. To protect the cliffs from erosion and to provide a safe place to unload catches the residents of Cromer have a long history of building piers and jetties. These have been built and rebuilt at Cromer since 1391 with almost countless instances of their destruction by storms, and an ongoing need to levy dues and taxes to pay for their rebuilding.

As well as the threat from the sea, Cromer fishermen in medieval days were in considerable danger from pirates. In 1404 fishermen from Cley and Cromer were granted the right to go to sea in convoy 'with forcible men, artillers and victuals to resist the King's enemies for the safety of the coasts and ports there'.

By the fifteenth century Cromer was a prosperous trading centre, its fishermen working waters off Norway, Denmark and Iceland for cod, herring, ling and orgeys. Cromer was also becoming well known for its crabs and lobsters. Daniel Defoe, in the eighteenth century, mentions both Cromer's fame for lobsters and its reputation as a dangerous coast for ships. This area of the Norfolk coastline became known as the 'Devil's Throat' because of the number of ship wrecks and lack of any safe harbour between here and Yarmouth.

Cromer has been a holiday resort since the late 1700s. Jane Austin in her novel *Emma* written in 1816 declares, 'Percy was a week at Cromer once, and he holds it to be the best of all the sea-bathing places.' There were two key factors in the development of Cromer from a rather exclusive and fashionable place for shooting, horse riding on the beach and sea-bathing by families of London gentry to the popular seaside resort of late Victorian days. The first was the coming of the railways in 1877. The second was the writing of Clement Scott, a journalist with the *Telegraph* and author, who popularised the Cromer coast as 'Poppyland' during the 1880s.

By 1900, with its new pier, promenade and many large hotels, the Hotel de Paris being one of the few which remains, it had all the trimmings of a holiday resort for the masses. The coming of the railway marked the end of an era. No longer did the two-masted sailing ships land their cargoes of Sunderland coal on the beach with the bustle of horse and donkey carts taking away the coal. Cromer was becoming a progressive new resort and one of the first in England to allow mixed bathing rather than the strict segregation of the sexes typical of the time. Modern Cromer, the holiday resort, had been born.

Opposite left: **Crab pots** – Cromer has a long history of crab fishing.
Opposite right: **Cromer crabs.**
Opposite below: **Cromer beach** – a tractor reverses pushing a crab boat towards the water.

FLOTSAM AND JETSAM

~ What's in a name? Cromer was once known as Crowsmere literally meaning the pond of Crows. Cromer is not mentioned in the Domesday book as at this time, in the eleventh century, a settlement existed north of the site of modern Cromer. This was the town of Shipden, lost to the sea through cliff erosion by the end of the fourteenth century.

~ The bells, the bells. Legend has it that the Church bells of the lost town of Shipden can still be heard in stormy weather from Cromer's seafront and herald disasters at sea.

~ A pier of two halves. In November 1993 the runaway rig, *Tayjack*, broke lose from its moorings off East Runton and was swept by a north-westerly gale into Cromer pier cutting a 30-metre hole through the pier at its landward end. The pier was repaired within a few months but the legal action to sort out who should pay took longer – six years!

~ The ghosts of Cromer Pier. Every theatre has its ghosts but the Pavilion Theatre on Cromer Pier has more than most. So many strange reports, from sightings of medieval men in rags to ghostly lifeboat men have been made that paranormal investigators have researched the pier. Whatever your beliefs it's certainly a place with strong atmospheres and a remarkable history.

~ The case of Black Shuck and Sherlock Holmes. North Norfolk's most terrifying spook haunts the cliffs between Sheringham, Cromer and Overstrand. Black Shuck is a huge, black hound with terrible blazing eyes who prowls the coastline at night. As the old Norfolk saying reports, 'And a dreadful thing from the cliff did spring, and its wild bark thrilled around. His eyes had the glow of fires below, 'twas the form of the Spectre Hound.' It's certainly not good news to meet Black Shuck as it's said that anyone who does will die within the year. Some say the myth goes back to Viking times and he is the embodiment of Shukr, the dog companion of the god Thor. Sir Arthur Conan Doyle visited Cromer in 1901 staying at Cromer Hall. He would undoubtedly have heard the local tales of Black Shuck and his 1902 best-seller, *Hound of the Baskervilles*, is clearly based on the story. Even Baskerville Hall in the book, while set on Dartmoor, bears a striking resemblance to Cromer Hall.

~ Cromer crabs. Cromer crabs have been famed for centuries as the best in Britain. Since medieval times they were traded from Cromer to the London markets. Today the crab boats still work from Cromer beach. The crabbing season is from April to September and each boat manages up to 200 pots with a two-man crew. The present Cromer Crab Company employs more than 150 people and supplies Cromer crabs across Europe. This company together with Norfolk Shellfish based in Sheringham handles over three million crabs a year!

~ Cromer beds. Cromer has given its name to the Cromer Forest Bed – an Ice Age deposit rich in fossils which outcrops in the cliffs – and to a period in Ice Age history, the Cromerian, for which Cromer's glacial cliff deposits are the best example.

~ The first Lifeboat station in Norfolk. Cromer has a long and proud history of lifeboats and lifeboatmen. Norfolk's very first lifeboat station was established here by public subscription in 1805. The most famous Cromer lifeboatman was Henry Blogg. He joined the lifeboat service in 1894 aged 18 only retiring 54 years later. He was coxswain through two world wars and won the RNLI's gold medal three times and silver medal four times, a unique achievement. Many sailors owe their lives to him and his crews and the daring rescues he led are legendary.

Opposite: **Sunset at Cromer pier.**

WILDERNESS AND WILDLIFE

Cliff slopes engraved in golden gorse
Above a beach etched white with breaking waves

Walk along Cromer pier and you walk above the least known wilderness of the North Norfolk coast. The seabed, below low water, is as rich and varied a habitat as any on dry land. More than 100 species of fish and marine invertebrates depend on these shallow inshore waters. Cromer is famous for its crabs for good reason: the seabed here, for several kilometres offshore, is littered with large flints. Crevices, nooks and crannies in this rocky underwater world make ideal homes for crabs and lobsters and support a tremendous diversity of other marine life.

These shallow waters are a highly threatened wilderness. The coastal waters of the North Sea remain productive but over-fishing has seen populations, first of herring, then of cod and mackerel, decimated. Other threats to wildlife include pollution and offshore sand and gravel extraction but most of all our marine wildlife suffers from our 'out of sight, out of mind' attitude. Although these marine creatures are as beautiful and fascinating as any, conservation organisations in general have been slow to take action to safeguard them.

Back on dry land Cromer has one of the most attractive cliff top walks of any in North Norfolk. Head east towards the lighthouse and within a few minutes walk there are cliff top woodlands and hidden, bracken covered valleys. In spring both the valley and the woods below the lighthouse are washed purple-mauve with carpets of bluebells. The cliffs east of Cromer have a completely different character from those between Weybourne and Sheringham. They are higher, reaching over 200 ft (70 metres), are generally less steep and almost entirely clothed in vegetation. There are acres of vivid yellow gorse which on sunny days scent the air with a heady coconut aroma. Kestrels and sparrowhawks regularly hunt along the cliffs here. Sand martins, swallows and swifts perform aerobatics sometimes flashing past just feet from cliff top walkers.

In Cromer take special note of the collared doves which are common in most large gardens here. In 1955 the pair which nested near Cromer was the first ever to breed in Britain. A Cromer wildlife success story! These pioneer birds were the forefront of an invasion which has made the collared dove a common bird through the whole country today.

Opposite: **Poppyland – the vibrant red of poppies brightens a field inland of Cromer.**
Above: **A waxwing in a Cromer garden – in some winters these birds arrive in numbers along the North Norfolk coast and are attracted to sites, including town gardens, that offer a plentiful supply of berries.**

Wildness is a quality in short supply in the modern world. The North Norfolk coast has this elusive quality in abundance. While we may not be able to define exactly what we mean by wildness there is something about the open landscapes – saltmarshes, sandflats, changing seascapes and huge skies – that we respond to. This wilderness quality is precious and deserves to be celebrated, valued and protected.

It may seem that the wildlife and wild places along the coast are well protected. A history of the British wildlife conservation movement could almost be written by tracing the diversity of conservation designations and range of conservation organisations at work here.

A string of nature reserves around the coast exemplifies the work of English Nature, RSPB, National Trust and Norfolk Wildlife Trust. The Wildlife Trust movement was born here when the Norfolk Naturalists' Trust (today's Norfolk Wildlife Trust) was established in 1926 and acquired its now famous reserve at Cley. RSPB's most visited reserve is the nationally-renowned Titchwell reserve. The first publicly owned reserve in Norfolk and one of the earliest reserves in England was created when the National Trust acquired Blakeney Point and the surrounding marshes in 1912. One of the earliest national nature reserves in the country was Scolt Head Island designated in 1954.

Yet nature reserves, with their defined and limited boundaries, can offer little long term protection to wildlife from the threat of climate change and rising sea levels. RSPB's Titchwell reserve with its narrow and eroding sand dune barrier is highly threatened by storm surges and rising sea level. The freshwater reedbeds and marshes at Cley, flooded by the sea in 1996, are unlikely to be sustainable for much longer in their present form.

The North Sea is in world terms a small, shallow, enclosed and extremely busy sea. The shipping, oil production and fishing industries of many nations are active here and no coastal reserve is immune from the consequences of a major oil spill or pollution incident. The impact of offshore gravel extraction on local marine life and its effects on coastal erosion is not yet fully understood. Even less predictable is the impact of a major wind farm to be developed off Cromer in the coming years.

Despite these threats, I am an optimist by nature. If we value the special qualities of North Norfolk's landscape and wildlife enough, then future generations will enjoy as rich, varied and beautiful an environment as we do today. Although, the one thing which conservation cannot achieve, even if it was desirable, is to keep the coast the same. To know even a little of the history of this coastline is to appreciate the sheer magnitude of changes which have occurred to both the human and natural elements of the area. Walk the coastline on any day and in any season and you will experience and be part of this ceaseless process of change.

The future for conservation will undoubtedly lie with allowing natural changes to occur. The overall pattern and fabric of wild places, wildlife and wild habitats cannot be protected by preventing change but is likely to be best maintained by working with nature's processes and allowing habitats to evolve. Rising sea levels may mean the sacrifice of some of the freshwater grazing lands, allowing saltmarshes to develop in their place. Saltmarshes are nature's sea defences and, unlike the land behind sea walls, are able to trap silt and build in height, keeping pace with rising sea levels.

The challenge for the future is to ensure that whatever changes do occur, the quality of the environment for both people and wildlife is protected. For centuries the prosperity of North Norfolk depended on the wealth generated through fishing and farming. Today, while fewer people are directly employed in these traditional industries, the prosperity of the area remains directly linked to its natural environment. More than two million visitors a year come to North Norfolk, drawn here, at least in part, by its natural beauty, wildlife and cultural heritage. Tourism is vital to its economy. The conundrum is how to ensure that visitor pressure doesn't kill the goose that lays the golden egg. If tourism can become a force for ensuring that the rich and varied landscapes, rare wildlife and the area's heritage of magnificent flint churches and fascinating history are valued and protected, then much will have been achieved. If visitors take away a deeper respect and understanding for the area's special nature then perhaps there will be wider benefits to both people and wildlife.

IN-CONCLUSION

The story of the North Norfolk coast is one with no beginning, no end, and certainly with no conclusions. This book therefore ends with an 'in-conclusion'.

This book is a celebration, through Martin's photos, of just a few of the special places and special landscapes of North Norfolk. The hardest part in writing it has been deciding what to leave out. The illustrations and words touch just a few of the elements of the North Norfolk coast and present two people's interest, passion and love for the area we are both lucky enough to live and work in.

One of the many joys of the area is that you don't have to travel to special designated nature reserves to enjoy its rich and varied wildlife. To chance on a barn owl quartering a field at sunset, watch a great skein of geese beat into the wind across a stormy sky, listen to a skylark in full song overhead or enjoy a road bank brightened by primroses and the spikes of early purple orchids is simply part of life here.

The human landscape is just as rich and varied. It's almost impossible to travel more than a few miles without turning a corner to discover a flint-walled church, stumble across an overgrown milestone, or wonder at the significance of a sunken green lane or the history of a sea wall and the land it encloses. Almost every village has a village sign decorated with clues to its local history and fortunately many have a pub where you can wonder whether stories of former smuggling have any truth.

There is a real danger that with the pace and pressures of a busy modern life we cease, almost without realising, to take the time to notice and enjoy this heritage. Enjoy the book, but even more importantly, enjoy North Norfolk.

173

Right: **A surprise around every corner – a scarecrow guards a North Norfolk field.**

APPENDIX

CONSERVATION ORGANISATIONS AND NATURE RESERVES

Wildlife on the North Norfolk coast is protected by nature reserves managed by several different organisations. This appendix provides contact details for the main conservation bodies and visiting details for the larger wildlife reserves. Be aware that visiting details and even phone numbers may change. The information is correct at the date of publication (September 2004).

CONSERVATION ORGANISATIONS:

English Nature (EN)
English Nature Norfolk Team
60 Bracondale
Norwich
NR1 2BE
Tel: 01603 598400
Website: www.english-nature.org.uk

National Trust (NT)
National Trust East of England Regional Office
Angel Corner
8 Angel Hill
Bury Saint Edmunds
Suffolk
IP33 1UZ
Tel: 0870 609 5388
Website: www.nationaltrust.org.uk

Norfolk Ornithologists Association (NOA)
Broadwater Road
Holme next the Sea
Hunstanton
Norfolk
PE36 6LQ
Tel: 01485 525406
Website: www.noa.org.uk

Norfolk Wildlife Trust (NWT)
Bewick House
22 Thorpe Road
Norwich
NR1 1RY
Tel: 01603 625540
Website: www.wildlifetrust.org.uk/norfolk

Royal Society for Protection of Birds (RSPB)
Eastern England Office
Stalham House
65 Thorpe Road
Norwich
NR1 1UD
Tel: 01603 661662
Website: www.rspb.org.uk

NATURE RESERVES:

These are listed from west to east along the coast.

Snettisham RSPB reserve
Map reference: TF652299
Facilities: Car park, birdwatching hides.
Opening times: Dawn to dusk (all year).
Information: Reserve leaflet, events programme and birdwatching tide tables available from RSPB.
Charges: Car park charge for non RSPB members.
Disabled access: By prior arrangement there is car access to hides suitable for disabled visitors.
Contact details: RSPB warden. Tel: 01485 542689

Holme Dunes NWT reserve
Map reference: TF715449
Facilities: Car park, birdwatching hides, visitor centre with small shop.
Opening times: Reserve open all year (except Christmas Day). The visitor centre is open daily, 10am to 5pm from Easter to October and at weekends from November to March.
Information: Reserve leaflet and events programme available from NWT.
Charges: Reserve entry charge. Free to NWT members and children.
Disabled access: One birdwatching hide is accessible for disabled visitors.
Contact details: The Warden, Holme Dunes National Nature Reserve, The Firs, Broadwater Road, Holme next the Sea, PE36 6LQ. Tel:01485 525240

Holme NOA Reserve and Bird Observatory
Map reference: TF715448
Facilities: Car park, birdwatching hides.
Opening times: 10am to 5pm daily (dawn to dusk NOA members).
Charges: Reserve entry charge. Free entry to NOA members.
Disabled access: Boardwalk and one birdwatching hide (Redwell hide) with disabled access.
Contact details: Jed Andrews, Broadwater Road, Holme next the Sea, Hunstanton, Norfolk, PE36 6LQ. Tel: 01485 525406

Titchwell Marsh, RSPB reserve
Map reference: TF750437
Facilities: Car park, toilets, visitor centre, shop, servery (hot drinks and snacks), birdwatching hides.
Opening times: Reserve open at all times. Visitor centre and shop: daily 9.30am to 5pm (9.30am to 4pm November to February). Closed 25, 26 December.
Information: Reserve leaflet and events programme available from RSPB.
Charges: Free entry to reserve, charge made for car parking.
Disabled access: Visitor centre, three hides and paths suitable for people in wheelchairs. Toilets for the disabled.
Contact details: Titchwell Marsh RSPB reserve, Titchwell, Norfolk, PE31 8BB. Tel: 01485 210779

Scolt Head Island (English Nature)
Map reference: TF815463
Facilities: Nature trail with interpretation boards.
Opening times: Dawn to dusk.
Information: Information leaflet available from English Nature.
Charges: Boat charge. No landing/entry charge to reserve. Access is by boat from Burnham Overy Staithe and Brancaster Staithe. Service is irregular and available April to September only. There is no access to the tern breeding colonies during the nesting season.
Disabled access: No provision.
Contact details: English Nature Norfolk Team. Tel: 01603 598400

174

Holkham (English Nature/Holkham Estate)

Map Reference: TF891448
Facilities: Car park, boardwalks, birdwatching hides.
Opening times: Reserve open at all times.
Information: Reserve leaflet available from English Nature.
Charges: Car parking charge on Lady Ann's Drive.
Disabled access: There is wheelchair access to one birdwatching hide (Washington hide) along the track on the inland side of the pines and a boardwalk gives access to a coastal viewpoint.
Contact details: English Nature. Tel: 01603 598400

Holkham Park (Holkham Estate)

Map reference: TF893435
Facilities: Car park, deer park and grounds. There are a range of facilities associated with the Hall and Estate including nursery gardens, history of farming museum, Bygones museum, arts, crafts and fine food centre, pottery shop and Stables café.
Opening times: Deer park and grounds open everyday except Christmas day.
Information: Leaflets and event details available from Holkham Estate.
Charges: Free entry to Park. Entry charge to Hall and Museums.
Disabled access: Good views of deer and woodland from surfaced pathways.
Contact details: Holkham Hall, Wells-next-the-Sea, Norfolk, NR23 1AB. Tel: 01328 710227
Email: enquiries@holkham.co.uk

Morston Marshes (NT)

Map reference: TG006442
Facilities: Car park, toilets, tower viewpoint, and information centre. Snacks and drinks available from servery during busy summer period (irregular hours).
Opening times: Access to marshes and coast path throughout year. Tower viewpoint and toilets open in summer only.
Information: No current site leaflet.
Charges: Pay and display car park (free to NT members)
Disabled access: Limited. There is wheelchair access to viewpoints across the marshes.

Contact details: NT Morston information centre – Tel: 01263 740174 (only open during busy summer periods, irregular hours depending on tides).
Further details: NT East Anglia regional office – Tel: 0870 609 5388

Blakeney Point (NT)

Map reference: TG997460
Facilities: Information centre in old lifeboat station and toilets (open 9am – 5pm April – September), one birdwatching hide.
Opening times: Reserve open dawn to dusk throughout year.
Information: Reserve guide available from NT.
Charges: Free entry to reserve.
Disabled access: No facilities on Blakeney Point.
Contact details: NT Blakeney Point warden, Tel: 01263 740480 (April – September), NT office Blakeney – Tel: 01263 740241

Cley Marshes (NWT)

Map reference: TG054441
Facilities: Visitor centre, shop, toilets, car park, four birdwatching hides, boardwalks.
Opening times: Reserve open every day except Christmas Day. Visitor centre open daily April – October, 10am to 5pm. In November and early December the visitor centre is open Wednesday – Sundays, 10am – 4pm.
Information: Reserve leaflet available from NWT.
Charges: Entry charge to reserve. Children and NWT members free. When visitor centre is closed entry tickets available from Watcher's Cottage. (400 metres towards Cley village on coast road).
Disabled access: Visitor centre has toilets for the disabled, four hides with wheelchair access, excellent access to reedbeds and hides along boardwalk.
Contact details: NWT Cley Marshes visitor centre – Tel: 01263 740008.

Sheringham Park (NT)

Map reference: TG139413
Facilities: Car park, visitor centre with small gift shop and servery with covered eating area (open from autumn 2004), toilets, way marked trails.
Opening times: Park – dawn to dusk all year.
Information: Map and leaflet available from NT.
Charges: Car parking charge (free to NT members).
Disabled access: Visitor centre with toilets for disabled, main routes partly accessible to wheelchair users, powered mobility vehicles available.
Contact details: NT Sheringham Park, Upper Sheringham, NR26 8TB. Tel: 01263 821429

Felbrigg Woods and Estate (NT)

Map reference: TG194394
Facilities: Car park, toilets, gardens, shop, tea-room, restaurant.
Opening times: Woodland and parkland walks open all year, dawn to dusk. Other facilities have variable weekday opening times depending on season but shop, tea-room and restaurant are open most weekends throughout the year.
Information: Walks map and leaflet available from NT
Charges: Free entry to Park and woodland walks. Charge for car parking (free to NT members)
Disabled access: Toilets for disabled, some routes wheelchair accessible.
Contact details: NT Felbrigg, Norwich, NR11 8PR. Tel: 01263 837444

BIBLIOGRAPHY

Arnott, K. (2000)
Hunstanton. The Story of a Small Norfolk Seaside Resort
Borough Council of King's Lynn and West Norfolk

Barringer, C. and Wright, J. (2002)
Blakeney in the Eighteenth Century
Blakeney Area Historical Society

Bloomfield, A. (1993)
Birds of the Holkham Area
Andrew Bloomfield

Bourne, U. (2003)
East Anglian Village and Town Signs
Shire Publications Ltd.

Brandon-Cox, H. (2002)
Mud on My Boots. The Estuaries and Countryside of the Norfolk Heritage Coast
East Countryman

Brooks, P. (1996)
Weybourne. Peaceful Mirror of a Turbulent Past
Poppyland Publishing

Brooks, P. (1998)
Cley. Living with Memories of Greatness
Poppyland Publishing

Brooks, P. (2002)
Sheringham. The Story of a Town
Poppyland Publishing

Brooks, P. (2001)
Blakeney. Have you heard about Blakeney?
Poppyland Publishing

Bridges, EM. (1998)
Classic Landforms of the North Norfolk Coast
The Geographical Society

Champion, M. (2000)
Seahenge. A Contemporary Chronicle
Barnwell's Timescape Publishing

Clarke, P. and M. (1987)
Where to Watch Birds in East Anglia
Christopher Helm, London

Dymond, D. (1990)
The Norfolk Landscape
The Alastair Press

Fiddian, V. (Ed) (2003)
Salthouse. The Story of a Norfolk Village
The Salthouse History Group

Hipper, K. (2001)
Smugglers All. Centuries of Norfolk Smuggling
The Larks Press

Leake, K. (1988)
East and West Runton
Poppyland Publishing

Mabey, R. (1990)
Home Country
Century

Margeson, S. (1997)
The Vikings in Norfolk
Norfolk Museums Service

Norfolk Federation of Women's Institutes (1999)
The Norfolk Village Book
Countryside Books

North, D. (1993)
Wilderness Walks
The Larks Press

Robinson, B. (1986)
The Peddars Way and Norfolk Coast Path
HMSO (Countryside Commission)

Rye, J. (1991)
A Popular Guide to Norfolk Place-names
The Larks Press

Stibbons, P. and Cleveland, D. (2001)
Poppyland. Strands of Norfolk History
Poppyland Press

Skipper, K. (2001)
Hidden Norfolk
Countryside Books

Taylor, M. (1987)
The Birds of Sheringham
Poppyland Publishing

Taylor, M. Seago, M. Allard, P. Dorling, D. (1999)
The Birds of Norfolk
Pica Press

Vesey, B. (2001)
The Hidden Places of East Anglia
Travel Publishing Ltd

Wade Martins, P. (1997)
An Historical Atlas of Norfolk
Norfolk Museums Service

Warren, M. (1994)
Cromer. The Chronicle of a Watering Place
Poppyland Publishing

Yaxley, S. (1986)
Sherringhamia The Journal of Abbot Upcher
The Larks Press

176

ACKNOWLEDGEMENTS

Many thanks to Mary Seal Coon, Paul and Dee Knapp, David and Hilary Tottman, Simon Rummery, Tasha North and Caroline Lister for reading and commenting on drafts of the text. Many errors of fact and punctuation have fortunately been weeded out through their efforts! The errors that remain are all my own.

I would also like to acknowledge my huge debt to the many authors listed in the bibliography. The knowledge I have gained from this background reading has added immensely to my own understanding and interest in the North Norfolk coast. Special thanks are owed to The Larks Press for permission to use information from *A Popular Guide to Norfolk Place-names* and to Ken Arnott whose book *Hunstanton. The Story of a Small Norfolk Seaside Resort* was invaluable for the Hunstanton section. My gratitude also goes to Carole McDonald and the team at Butler and Tanner for their guidance and design skills in the production of this book.

Finally I would like to thank Tasha and Dominic for their support during the lengthy gestation and birth of the book. It would not have been possible without them.